Mathability (math + ability)

"They can, because they think they can."

—Virgil

Nothing is more important. In today's increasingly complex and technological world the most important thing you can do for your child is to nurture mathability. It is an attitude. Those who say 'that their child is poor at maths' are doing themselves an injustice. They are undermining the child's future.

Mathability is a skill that teaches a child how to think. Mathability is a skill that develops the inherent intelligence potential. It enhances problem solving abilities and analytical focus. The methods and the techniques are just as suitable for adults as for children. Indeed many of the methods have altered the mindset even of senior executives and housewives.

To something that is often subjected to complexity, confusion and prejudices, Shakuntala Devi brings clarity, simplicity and practicality. She corrects many of the generally held misconceptions and effectively demostrates how mathability is an acquired skill.

Nurture Mathability. Nurture Success.

The Author

Born in a well-known family of Brahmin priests in Bangalore, Shakuntala Devi received her early lessons in mathematics from her grandfather. By the age of five, she was recognised as a child prodigy and an expert in complex mental arithmetic. A year later she demonstrated talents to a large assembly of students and professors at the University of Mysore.

Hailed as an authentic heroine of our times her feats are recorded in the *Guiness Book of World Records*. She has made international headlines for out-performing and out-computing the most sophisticated computers in the world.

She maintains that a child's curiosity and receptivity during infancy and childhood can never be matched, and we must, as parents, nurture the young minds by offering the right learning process and motivation to develop the innate strengths possessed by every child.

These days she spends most of her time giving shape to her dreams of setting up a gigantic mathematical institute for teaching and research in maths.

MATHABILITY

Awaken the Math Genius in Your Child

SHAKUNTALA DEVI

Orient
Paperbacks

DELHI | MUMBAI | HYDERABAD

How to Order

This book is also available on special quantity discounts from the publisher Orient Paperbacks, 5A/8 First Floor, Ansari Road, Darya Ganj, New Delhi-110 002. Tel.: +91-11-2327 8877, Fax: +91-11-2327 8879 e-mail: mail@orientpaperbacks.com. On your business letterhead, kindly include information concerning the intended use of the books and the number of copies you wish to purchase.

www.orientpaperbacks.com

ISBN 13: 978-81-222-0316-5
ISBN 10: 81-222-0316-7

1st Published 2002
10th Printing 2010

Mathability: Awaken The Math Genius in Your Child

© Shakuntala Devi

Cover design by Vision Studio

Published by
Orient Paperbacks
(A Division of Vision Books Pvt. Ltd.)
5A/8 Ansari Road, New Delhi-110 002

Printed in India at
Saurabh Printers Pvt. Ltd., Noida

Cover Printed at
Ravindra Printing Press, Delhi-110 006

Contents

1

Of Maths and Mathematicians

Prejudice is the child of ignorance.
WILLIAM HAZLITT

*T*he merry-go-round whirled in a kaleidoscope
of colours. The giant wheel turned majesti-
cally on its axis. Lights blazed and the loud-
speaker blared music and announcements alter-
nately. All around me voices buzzed and squealed.
The crowd pushed, hustled and bustled. If I were
to count and note down the number of times I
was nudged sharply by impatient elbows I'm
sure it would be a statistician's delight! The funfair
was in full swing and I allowed myself to be
carried from stall to stall by the sheer surge and
swell of the crowd.

'Come and see the fattest woman in the
world!' a voice chanted, and coaxed us towards
a huge white tent. I stood and stared at the
monstrous woman clad in a strange, sequinned,
garish outfit. Rolls of fat bulged from her body,

making her look like an inhuman mass. There were nudges and sniggers as the group viewed this 'freak'. Saddened, I turned away and was on my way out of the tent, when two clear voices in conversation made me falter in my stride.

'Poor woman! She's really a freak of nature, isn't she?' said a middle-aged woman.

'She's just a fat lady,' replied the man with her. 'Nothing freakish about that. I think scientists, mathematicians, and artists are the original freaks. Mental freaks!'

There was something deliberate about his tone that made me realise that he had recognised me!

Maths: Mixed reactions, strong emotions

I have, by now, become used to the varied reactions that greet me. Sometimes it's unnerving. Even with my considerable mental ability with numbers, I'm still not clear on one point: whether being a mathematician has more pluses or minuses! Perhaps every profession has its share of strange reactions. I know a doctor who, when on vacation, refrains from prefixing his name with 'Dr'. 'The moment an acquaintance comes to know I'm doctor, I have to listen to a list of all his aches and pains!' he says with a comical lift of his eyebrow. 'And there goes my holiday!'

A writer friend has quite another tale to tell. A brigadier moved next door to him. My friend being of a friendly disposition, invited him to his house for a neighbourly drink.

'What do you do?' asked the brigadier, as they toasted their budding friendship.

10

'I write,' replied my friend. 'I'm a writer.'

'I see,' said the good brigadier, puzzled. 'But what do you *do*? Don't you have a profession?'

You'd think that in this world where the sciences are respected, a mathematician would be considered the *creme de la creme* of society. Not that I have never experienced this feeling. I have. When people realise I'm a mathematician, I *do* see a spark of respect. But not always. A mathematician's image, I'm afraid, is fogged by a hotchpotch of numerals, symbols, and fractions. A computer instead of a person ... dry, dusty, unattractive ... coldly clinical, who peers at the world through grey-tinted glasses... dressed like a tramp.

Mathematicians: Talented, gifted, but . . .

A little girl once, remarked, 'Why! You are nice!'

'Thank you,' I said amused.

'My mom told me I should behave myself and not act silly and giggly with you,' she went on with childlike candour. 'But she was wrong! You laughed at *all* my jokes!'

How refreshing it was to hear that! The little girl was right. Mathematicians *can* laugh. How I wish that adults were as open-minded as that child. Most people slot mathematicians into a pigeonhole of preconceived ideas. They assume that I want to be always addressed as 'madam', that I don't know a thing about life outside the pages of my numerological epistles! I've met people who, when introduced to me, say 'Hello' and then fidget uneasily. I can see what is going on in their minds: 'What do I say to a mathematician?' It is as if I am a being from another planet who doesn't even talk the same language!

I've had such remarks thrown at me:

'I'm a "dummy" at maths!'

'Could you teach my son some tricks to make him pass his maths exam?'

'God, you're lucky! You must always know exactly how much change you have to get when you buy something!'

'Beyond knowing two plus two makes four, I'm zero!'

'Do you have any time for hobbies?'

'Don't you ever get bored?'

When they get to know me, people are surprised that I'm human too! That I have a sense of humour. And that I can talk about food, family, music, films ...

A mathematician is usually known by two initials — BB: Brilliant and Boring! The 'boring' is part of a self-defence mechanism that stems from the other person's own feelings of inferiority. It is a strange social phenomenon. For some inexplicable reason, mathematics is seen as an exalted cloud on which only a chosen few reside. What it lacks is glamour.

For this reason, the mathematician finds himself or herself in a no-win situation. Talented, gifted, great for a maths quiz show perhaps, but not interesting enough to have a cup of tea with!

I suppose it has something to do with the aura surrounding the persona. A film personality has an aura of glamour and glitter. A saint has an aura of spirituality and humanity. Both have an 'otherworldly' halo attached to them. But the mathematician's aura is unfortunately seen more as a combination of musty figures and boring calculations! How often have you heard of a mathematician being interviewed for a magazine article? I think the weakness lies in the fact that there has been almost no attempt to make mathematics 'people-oriented'. It is viewed exactly as it is defined in the dictionary: *an abstract science of space and numbers.* Where are the emotions, the culture, the human angles, the highs and lows, the conflicts, and the drama that draw people to a subject? Where are the anecdotes that give flesh and blood to the most abstract of theories or thoughts?

First impressions:
Mmm ... mathematics, ugh ... mathematics

I asked a friend about her earliest recollections of mathematics. I'm quoting her verbatim because I think her words provide a piercing insight into the misconceptions about maths imbibed in childhood:

'Initially, maths was an easy affair. My mother would place first one apple in front of me and then another. So I knew that one plus one equalled two, and so on. I graduated to fractions. She'd cut the apple, and I learnt about "half" and "quarter". But my problems with maths began in school. My father now entered the picture. He insisted that I get full marks in maths. This jolted me. Suddenly, the subject I had enjoyed became a burden. My maths teacher was a stern old man, always dressed in an ill-fitting, rumpled, grey-checked jacket and brown trousers. He'd call each of us to the front of the class to work out a sum on the blackboard. If we did it right, he'd say, "I knew you were a clever girl." But if we got it wrong, he'd say, "Bad girl!" and banish us to the back of the class. I'd approach the blackboard every day with the terrible fear of being publicly labelled "bad". It was a humiliating experience.'

The negative approach of a parent or teacher with high expectations, without the element of fun, drives the child away from what is really an interesting subject.

The first impression remains with the child even as he or she matures into adulthood. When the child is fed a new titbit, her first reaction is to spit it out because of the foreign taste. Sometimes, the 'bad taste' remains. So it is with mathematics. It has left a bad taste in the mouths of a majority of people. The almost paranoic distaste of maths is transferred to the mathematician. But I hope I can change that image.

Mathematics is a fascinating subject. In the next chapter, I've attempted to lift the iron curtain, metaphorically speaking, to give you a glimpse into the more human aspect of it. With a better understanding and a more human approach, I am sure you can influence yourself and your child to change that 'sickening, mushy' stuff into something that is enjoyable, delicious and crunchy. By the end of this book, I hope you will be saying: 'Mmm … mathematics!'

2
Maths in Everyday Life

Nothing has changed but my attitude.
Everything has changed.
ANTHONY DEMELLO

I've met more people who profess a hatred for maths than those who are indifferent to it. For some reason, the subject is like a red rag in front of them. Social graces are dropped, as such maths haters tell me with a shiver of distaste, 'Maths is boring.' Initially, I found it strange. I couldn't imagine walking up to a history professor, for instance, and telling him: 'History is boring.' Not that I find any subject tedious, but the point I am trying to make is that social etiquette demands a certain diplomacy. Maths seems to strip away that veneer to show the snarl beneath. It puzzled me, until I attended an advertising workshop.

Smartly clad, articulate executives spoke about 'upmarket advertising', 'brand loyalty', 'market-leadership', and so on. They projected slides to demonstrate or prove a certain point, or even to create an interest. One gentleman spoke at length about marketing a soap to a specified target audience. Communication was touched upon. There was a discussion on products endorsed by celebrities. I went home with all the advertising buzzwords running through my brain.

The idea hit me at around midnight. Now I knew why maths was so unpopular. Of course! It was so simple! Why hadn't I realized it earlier? Obviously, the subject had never been *marketed*! It was treated as a 'product'; it was of a high standard but it had no glossy packaging, nothing to recommend it. It had excellent salient features built into it, but millions of people all over the world were unaware of it. Mathematicians and teachers had made no attempt to communicate these exciting qualities. Literature, on the other hand, is a 'self-marketer'. Its essence lies in its communicative abilities. Maths needs to be marketed. Since it is taught using numerals and symbols, it is not so much a foreign language, as an alien one.

The language of symbols is alien to us since we don't use it in our everyday speech. We don't use it in our daily communication, except perhaps in a specific context.

The maths alien

This 'alien' feeling comes through clearly when a person meets a mathematician. The 'numbers person' is viewed as a different species. And since maths has the label of 'high intelligence' attached to it, the other person feels inferior. Predictably, he or she turns away, or is hostile. He cannot comprehend that 'this-person-who-deals-and-probably-thinks-in-symbols', is also a living, breathing, emotional human being with normal desires and aspirations. That the mathematician talks the same language, eats the same food, plays tennis, and listens to music, is ignored.

For many, 'maths-alienness' begins at home. A budding actor told me, 'I remember I had to sit at this huge dining table at home. My grandfather, who was a wizard at maths, would check my homework. If I made a mistake, he'd thunder at me. He considered me a failure because both he and my father had been whiz-kids. I was not seen as a chip of the two old blocks!' The human mind is a funny thing. Negative impressions made in childhood seem to remain imprinted on our minds forever. Parents with high expectations come down heavily on their children, driving them into a corner. Sometimes sibling rivalries are triggered off by obvious and unfair comparisons.

If you have had similar experiences, take them out and examine them. More often than not, you will find that your own maths-alienness arises not out of your 'natural' hatred for the subject, but from your disgust or rebellion against an authoritarian adult. If you can recognise that, you will already be on a new, exciting road strewn with fresh possibilities and opportunities. You may shrug and say, 'I've done without maths so far, I can do without it forever, thank you!' But look at it this way: why would you want to shut your mind to *anything*?

As natural as breathing

What I want you to do is to overcome your feeling of maths-alienness, if you have it. I want you to enjoy every moment of your life with maths. Maths may or may not play a large part in your life, but it is essential in every field. Whether you realise it consciously or not, you are breathing, living, even eating maths.

After all, you have to programme your day: wake up to an alarm, fix breakfast, catch the nine o'clock bus. When you exercise, you count the sets, check your pulse rate. You may be measuring your daily calorie intake. When you eat out, you glance at the right-hand side of the menu card to avoid ordering beyond your budget. You scan bills for accuracy before paying them. You balance your chequebook every week. When you listen to music, your mind absorbs the rhythmic (read: mathematical) beat. You time your oven, the pressure cooker. Statistics reported in newspapers interest you — like the number of runs scored by Sachin Tendulkar or Imelda Marcos' shoe collection! Or that in 1990, Evander Holyfield, the boxer, was the highest paid athlete in the world — his income totalling $ 60.5 million. Then, you may hear on the news that a 105-year-old man still lives on, hale and hearty. You may listen to the weather report to know at what temperature you are sweltering in!

By doing all this you are already tuned in to a fascinating mathematical world. It is as natural as breathing. You are already enjoying a major portion of it; why not enjoy *all* of it?

Your competitive edge

I've talked about everyday maths in your life. But even professionally, you may find that taking up a maths-oriented course gives you an edge over your colleague for a promotion. Or you may find that reading and analysing graphs gives you a better insight into your area of work. Even if maths doesn't come directly into your profession, you could land a job because of your interest in it!

Vijay was a chemist at a pharmaceutical factory for several years. Slowly, he began to feel he was in a rut. He scanned the wanted ads in the papers everyday. A company specialising in holding chemical exhibitions, called him for an interview. During the course of the interview, the proprietor asked Vijay about his hobbies. It so happened that Vijay was an amateur astronomer. Casually, he mentioned it as one of his hobbies.

19

The proprietor was electrified. He happened to be one himself too! The same day, Vijay walked out with his letter of appointment as a manager in the company.

So, you see, you never know what opportunities await you in this great, wide world! Why not make the best of them? You should not stop yourself from taking an excellent job simply because one of your duties may involve a little maths. The job may be perfect in every way. It could be the making of you. It could be 'The Dream Job' that would fulfil your interest, your aspirations, your ambitions. It may have a fabulous salary and unimaginable perks attached to it. Everything about it may be what you've hoped for, except for that one little clause.

There are two scenarios: one, you chicken out, in which case you've lost a great opportunity; two, you take it, but dread the maths part of it. Either way you are miserable. You curse yourself, your job, your boss, your colleagues.

But let me paint a third scenario for you. You decide to take the job. You are determined to tackle every duty with verve. You tell yourself, 'I'm going to enjoy totting up those figures!' or words to that effect. As you get deeper into it, your optimistic approach pays dividends. You find you *are* enjoying it. You realise that you never knew you had this talented side to you. You are more confident, more self-assured. You know now that you can tackle anything. You've joined the league of when-the-going-gets-tough-the-tough-get-going!

You are the master

It is extremely important not to allow a feeling of man-made maths-alienness shut off channels to wider vistas. For starters, change your outlook about maths. See it for what it is. Don't let a negative parental attitude influence your life today. Forget phrases like:

'I've got no head for figures.'

'I hate maths.'

'I can't stand the thought of balancing my chequebook!'

Just as you bundle up old refuse and throw it in the trash bin, so should you with your old, outdated fears. You are going to start afresh. No, you are never too old to learn a new thought process. Old Man Maths is not an ogre. He is a friend. Like a tried and tested horse, he is always at your beck and call, ready to be harnessed. It is up to you to take up the reins and guide him to wherever you want  him to go. Remember, he is not your master. You are the one in the saddle. You call the shots.

3

Origin of Maths: The Dynamic Numerals

*All acts performed in the world
begin in the imagination.*

BARBARA GRIZZUTI HARRISON

Who is the greatest, most brilliant
mathematician in the world? You won't
find him in the person-of-the-year list. You won't
see his or her name in the hallowed halls of fame.
The *person* I am referring to is: Mother Nature.
Are you surprised? And well may you be. After
all, you have normally viewed nature as the great
cosmic force which fills your world with beauty,
and, sometimes, disasters. But I am not talking
about flora and fauna. The breathtaking visions
that you see all around you, the artistic twirls,
the glowing colours, are all manifestations of a
natural law or plan laid out by nature with
mathematical precision!

It is nature's blueprint that charts the paths
of the stars and planets. Such is her precision,
that astronomers can know in advance the exact

location of these heavenly bodies at a given time. You can see the sun rising in the east and setting in the west as though it has been programmed. Similarly, seasons follow one another in perfect cycles.

And you, nature's child, ride on this great mathmagical current — ebbing, advancing, flowing with it. So, you see, mathematics surges through our very system. It is silent, never seen at work, and cannot be perceived through our five senses. That is the reason we have been unable to recognise it. It is too abstract, too intangible. When you watch a sunrise or a sunset, you are only seeing the result of this great intangible power.

The Indian Numeral System

I think this magic of numbers permeated into our ancestors. Somewhere in their minds, a seed was sown and began to flourish. Slowly, the ancient sages of India worked on and evolved a numeral system. Today, we have a name for it — the Decimal System. But for our great forefathers, it was a creative endeavour, a labour of love. Their thought process evolved on the basis that with only ten symbols — the ten fingers on their hands — they should be able to represent any number. It sounds so simple. It is, but only a brilliant brain could have developed it thus. The ten symbols are our basis for calculation even today. We call them numbers or digits. We write or read them as: 1, 2, 3, 4, 5, 6, 7, 8, 9, 0. These ten symbols stand for or are pronounced as: one, two, three, four, five, six, seven, eight, nine, and zero, respectively.

The sages didn't stop there. They took on the bigger challenge of positioning or placing these symbols. The far right position in any numeral became the unit. Moving left, the next position became ten. That is how we have ones, tens, hundreds, thousands, and so on. When we write these positions, they look like this:

1 (unit)

10

100

1000

The most exciting part of this positioning system is that it is so universal. Take a more complex number like 5081. How do you break it down?

$(\underline{5} \times 1000) + (\underline{0} \times 100) + (\underline{8} \times 10) + (\underline{1} \times 1) = 5081.$

Today, when we say, 'The price of this item is five thousand and eighty-one rupees,' it rolls off our tongues so easily. But it was our ancestors who made it possible for us to express ourselves in this way. We are able to put a value to the item and do not need to rely on the old, primitive barter system.

You can see this system at work graphically too. For example, take the figure of 37 and translate it into dots:

$\cdots \cdots \cdots = (10 \times 1)$ dots

$\cdots \cdots \cdots = (10 \times 1)$ dots

$\cdots \cdots \cdots = (10 \times 1)$ dots

$\cdots \cdots = (\ 7 \times 1)$ dots

You will notice that each line or group represents ten dots, except for the last one which has seven single dots. If you write it down, it would be:

$(3 \times 10) + (7 \times 1) = 37$

You will also find that there is an emphasis on tens. How did our forefathers come up with this magic figure of ten? As mentioned earlier, it is most likely that they relied on, or found a measure from the most flexible parts of their bodies — the ten fingers!

It is certainly food for thought, isn't it? Imagine the sheer ingenuity of man that made him work out an entire mathematical system from a part of his anatomy! Even today, you see people counting on their fingers.

It is important to understand the full impact of this thought process because only then will you begin to understand 'Old Man Mathematics'. He was born out of you, and you have him at your fingertips!

Sublimity and simplicity are the essence of our Indian civilization, of the wisdom and sagacity of our ancestors. Perhaps that is why it is so symbolic and fitting that the seeds of a singularly phenomenal science of mathematics should have sprung from India — a silent but dynamic science that stormed the world with its great possibilities.

The Arabic Numeral System

How fortunate for the human race that in those days there were no travel restrictions. Traders, merchants, and explorers crossed countries and sailed the vast oceans freely, bearing not only goods but also knowledge across borders. And so it came to pass that the Arabs learnt about the Indian Numeral System and adopted it as their own. The great chain of communication continued and reached the borders of Europe.

The Story of Zero

It is believed that the Hindu-Arabic symbols for numbers have been used as early as five or six centuries before the birth of Christ. In the earliest stages, however, the Hindu-Arabic system of number notation did not contain a symbol for zero. Without the zero the system was not of much use. The earliest known use of the Hindu-Arabic zero occurs in an Indian inscription dated 876. B.C. And the indisputable superiority of the Hindu-Arabic system over all others is a consequence of introducing the zero concept and symbol.

The word 'Cipher' means zero. 'Cipher', comes from the Arabic 'Sifr' and our word zero is derived from this word.

1. Any number plus zero equals the number.
2. Any number minus zero equals the number.
3. Zero minus any number equals the negative of the number.
4. Any number times zero equals zero.
5. Zero divided by any number except zero equals zero.
6. The operation of dividing by zero is not defined and is not permitted.

The earliest known 'maths merchants', instrumental in transmitting the Indian Numeral System from Arab sources, were Robert of Chester and Abelard of France in the twelfth century. The exciting new invention was well received in Europe, and was duly christened the Arabic Numeral System. Later, when it was discovered that it was of Indian origin, it came to be known as the Hindu-Arab system.

Evolution of Roman Numbers

The world of mathematics bubbles over with interesting stories. Unfortunately, our present day teachers rarely discuss the interesting human face of this wonderful science. For example, the ancient Romans had their own method. They converted letters to represent numbers, giving the Roman system its own identity. Thus, I stood for one; V stood for five; X stood for ten. In short:

$$I = 1$$
$$V = 5$$
$$X = 10$$

To give meaning to these alphabets, they devised a few simple, general rules:

1. Repeating a letter *doubles* its value:
   XX = 10 + 10 = 20

2. A letter placed after one of greater value *adds* to its value: VI = 5 + 1 = 6.

3. A letter placed before one of greater value *subtracts* from its value: IV = 5 – 1 = 4.

4. A dash over a numeral *multiplies* its value by a thousand: $\overline{X}$ = 10 × 1000 = 10,000.

How painstakingly, but logically, must the ancient Roman intellectuals have worked out this system! And how they must have rejoiced when they charted it to the end!

Thanks to the brilliance of Indian and Roman mathematicians, we have inherited two numeral systems. However, it is the Indian method that has prevailed. Interestingly, the Roman numerals are like a shorthand translation of the Indo-Arab numerals as their value increases, as you can see for yourself.

Many people have told me that they are nonplussed by high value Arabic numeral. A high-flying business tycoon once told me humorously, 'I have to be careful when I say "billion".' In the USA and France, a billion equals *a thousand million*, whereas in England, a billion is a *million-million*! Up to a point, India has her own

Indo-Arab (I/A) and Roman (R) Numerals							
I/A	R	I/A	R	I/A	R	I/A	R
1	I	11	XI	30	XXX	5000	$\overline{V}$
2	II	12	XII	40	XL	10,000	$\overline{X}$
3	III	13	XIII	50	L	50,000	$\overline{L}$
4	IV	14	XIV	90	XC	100,000	$\overline{C}$
5	V	15	XV	100	C	500,000	$\overline{D}$
6	VI	16	XVI	200	CC	1,000,000	$\overline{M}$
7	VII	17	XVII	400	CD		
8	VIII	18	XVIII	500	D		
9	IX	19	XIX	900	CM		
10	X	20	XX	1,000	M		

nomenclatures. For your entertainment, I've given, a table of higher Indian-Arabic numerals with their American and European counterparts:

Numeral Values Across the World			
Number	*USA/France*	*UK/Europe* (except France)	*India*
1&5 zeros	one hundred thousand	one hundred thousand	one lakh
1&6 zeros	million	million	ten lakh
1&7 zeros	ten million	ten million	one crore
1&8 zeros	hundred million	hundred million	ten crore
1&9 zeros	billion	milliard (thousand million)	hundred crore
1&12 zeros	trillion	billion (million million)	
1&15 zeros	quadrillion	thousand billion	
1&18 zeros	quintillion	trillion	
1&21 zeros	sextillion	thousand trillion	
1&24 zeros	septillion	quadrillion	
1&27 zeros	octillion	thousand quadrillion	
1&30 zeros	nonillion	quintillion	
1&33 zeros	decillion	thousand quintillion	

So, the next time you want to let off steam, try, 'I've told you a *quadrillion* times not to do this!' It is sure to get a reaction nonillion times over!

The Imperial System

The evolution and branching out of mathematics could be a cartoonist's delight. Yes, indeed, it has its own idiosyncracies! The primitive Anglo-Saxons had a rough and ready reference for measuring — their hands! But for obvious reasons, this method was undependable. And it wouldn't be wrong to say that one man's *inch* might be another man's *foot*! But they managed somehow, until they derived the Imperial System.

Though the new Imperial System was based on the old Anglo-Saxon one, an attempt was made to make it more uniform and exact in the British Empire. After much bone-cracking, the royal mathematicians decided that the *inch* was the length of the knuckle of the thumb!

King Edgar must have grumbled, 'Give them an inch and they take a yard!' The next thing he knew was that the *yard* was the distance from the tip of his royal nose to the tip of his majestic middle finger as he held his arm and hand outstretched!

Perhaps the mile proved to be a 'milestone' around their necks! Here, they decided to borrow from the Roman legionaries. The Roman *milli* was one thousand paces which, when measured, proved to be about 1618 yards. But paces varied, so the *mile* was eventually standardised at 1760 yards — a nice round figure.

Satisfied that they had taken the first step in the right direction, the math-men turned their minds to a larger area. I can quite imagine the Englishman standing with his lips pursed, gazing at the oxen bearing the yoke on their muscular shoulders, as they ploughed the land. As the sun began to set, he might have exclaimed, 'By Jove, I've got it!' And the *acre* was furrowed out by measuring the amount of land ploughed by the oxen in a day!

You have to admire the mathematician's immense observational powers and creativity in bringing some order to the Imperial System. English-speaking countries, including the USA, naturally adopted it.

The Metric System: *Systematic & deliberate*

France, however, evolved the Metric System in a more systematic, or deliberate manner. The *metre* was equalled to one-ten millionth of a quadrant of the earth's meridian. Napoleon gave it his stamp of approval and it was adopted by France and introduced to other European countries.

Of course, eventually, a more sophisticated approach was adopted and standardised. To give you an example, the metre is now defined as 'the length of the path travelled by light in vacuum during a time interval of 1/299, 792, 458 of a second.' Try that one out in your next family quiz contest!

Music of Maths

I've left the choicest bit to be savoured last. Mathematics, to use contemporary terminology, proved to be a user-friendly science. It led to the development of astronomy, physics, and other sciences. But if you think that it has been used only in the world of science, you will be surprised. Maths has dipped its talented fingers into the arts too. Western and Eastern music have their roots in mathematics.

On his way home one day, the great mathematician Pythagoras suddenly stopped and swivelled around. His keen ear had caught a delightful ring coming from a shop — a ring that seemed to have a certain rhythm and harmony to it. Eager to find the source, he peered inside, and what do you think he saw? Musicians? No. He saw five blacksmiths wielding their hammers on the anvil! As he watched and listened entranced, he observed that each hammer was of a different weight, and made a different sound as it thumped against the anvil. He soon realized that the heavy hammer produced a lower note than the lighter one. He frowned, feeling instinctively that there was something wrong: one hammer was not quite in sync with the others. It was slightly off-key, he felt. Tentatively he explained this to the blacksmiths and asked if he could borrow their hammers for an experiment. The humble men were surprised but agreed readily.

Back home, he weighed the tools individually. Each hammer yielded a different weight in a certain proportion to the next one, except for the 'off-key' hammer. When he corrected it to suit his calculations, he found that the rings were now in synchronization! By constant experimentation, he soon devised a musical scale!

An Indian classicist once told me, '*Talas* are simple arithmetic!' *Talas* are rhythmic cycles of a group of beats. For example, the *teentaal* has 16 beats divided into four groups each. It goes:

na-dhin-dhin-na/na-dhin-dhin-na/na-dhin-dhin-na/na-dhin-dhin-na.

1-2-3-4/5-6-7-8/9-10-11-12/13-14-15-16.

Mathematically, one could write it as:

$4 + 4 + 4 + 4 = 16$ or $4 \times 4 = 16$

One school of Indian music called *Carnatic* even harnesses fractions! Eventually, what we hear is a *measured* mix of sounds, which, when emphasised, slowed down, or accelerated produce pleasing rhythmic music! It would be too sweeping a statement to say music is maths or maths is music. But without a measured discipline, there would be no music — Western or Eastern — only a cacophony of sounds.

I hope I have succeeded in arousing your interest in the colourful culture of mathematics. Believe me, it is a wonderful world. In some ways, it is like learning a new language. It is challenging, stimulating and, for that very reason, fascinating. Like music, it has a wide range — from the minuscule atom to the vast skies and beyond. It has permutations and combinations that add to its dimension. Maths is a great subject. Don't knock it, just try it!

4

Maths is Essential For Success!

To know what has to be done, then do it, comprises the whole philosophy of life.
SIR WILLIAM OSLER

*D*ictators are viewed with distaste, hatred, suspicion ... yet parents themselves, more often than not, are dictators in their own homes. They turn their children's faces in the direction they feel is right for them. The strangest thing about this self-defeating exercise is that the direction is decided not on the basis of the aptitude of the child, but by the inclination of the parents.

The dictator uses his trained army to wield his power. Parents use their image as role models for the child, and the tiresome axiom of 'father knows best' to wield their power. Smiles and gentle words make this attitude no less objectionable. They only make it more palatable as they brainwash young minds.

Parents and relatives obviously influence a growing child's mind. Strangely enough, even teachers whose very profession consists of teaching maths, can make as big a mess as the parents. I find this astonishing, because teaching by its very nature should have good communication blended into it. The fact is that good mathematicians are rarely good communicators. I think maths courses should include the fine art of communication as a subject. This is very important as it would have a positive impact on our future generations. This way, both girls and boys would grow up with well-rounded personalities. At present, it is a one-dimensional mental growth, whichever way you look at it.

Maths should be enjoyed and understood, not shunned totally or taken as bitter medicine.

Some people I have spoken to blamed the personality of the maths teacher for having had a negative impact on them. For example, Rima, a homemaker, told me, 'My maths teacher was an awkward, bony, bespectacled spinster called Miss Nair. She had a funny walk, as though she had a hernia. I always had the fear that if I became proficient in maths, I'd become like her.'

Rima's outlook was immature and illogical. In fact, I feel sympathetic towards Miss Nair. She didn't fit the stereotype feminine model that has been pushed down our throats by society. That she taught a 'masculine' subject like maths probably added to it. Rima confessed that her mother and she would privately poke fun at this teacher. I didn't want to hurt Rima's feelings or I'd have told her that it was her mother, not Miss Nair, who was to blame. It was her mother who was perpetuating this narrow vision of a woman's role in society.

Another young woman called Lily had a more amusing anecdote to relate. She described her maths teacher as an old man whose clothes always smelt of mothballs. 'I related maths to that musty smell,' she concluded, 'and couldn't bear it.'

It is strange how unimportant, isolated little details or incidents can make or mar a child's interest in maths.

I hope through my book to influence more and more people to consider maths to be a friend,

equally accessible to both women and men. We are all blessed with brains and nobody is less intelligent than the other in sphere, including mathematics.

In some cultures while boys are often encouraged to study mathematics, and expected to master it, girls are subtly, diverted away from it, under the mistaken belief that it is not for them. Infact, speaking symbolically, I'd say that the first mathematician was a woman — Eve. Yes, Eve. She plucked *one* apple from the tree of knowledge and decided to go *halves* with Adam. The symbolism lies not only in the mathematical terms I've used, but in the larger context too. She plucked it from the tree of knowledge. She displayed a curiosity that is the very basis for imbibing any knowledge.

Maths: A success multiplier

One very exciting aspect of mathematics is its ever-evolving nature even as its foundation remains firm as a rock. It's like a tree with strong roots, whose branches spread wider and wider.

'Mathability', today, is not just confined to engineering, accounting, geology, computer programming or such technical fields. It has percolated down to various management fields as well. Earlier, an executive in a garment export firm may have been chosen because of his pleasant manners, his ability to handle clients, his knowledge of fabrics and fashions. Today, in addition, he is expected to handle 'data', 'statistics', and 'investigative graphs' do 'quantitative analyses', and 'target planning'.

A candidate who presents himself as ideal for a particular job has to have these technical skills. It is not enough that he is able to read export journals and magazines to keep up with the trends. He must be comfortable reading figures and 'thinking mathematically' as well.

With increasing competition in every field, analytical data is fast becoming as common as literature. If that sounds ridiculous, I assure you that even literacy was initially confined to a few until it gained universality. Mathematical-literacy has an important role in this high-tech age, and we must get our act together if we do not want to be left behind.

There is maths in everything. Maths is both the mother and child of all science and art. It is the heartbeat of learning, the alphabet of one school of knowledge. It is the foundation of all order. Even the simple 'two plus two equals four' formula gives us an exactness and yardstick. Without order, all would be chaos. Whether it is our heartbeats, words or chants, music or *mantras*, maths permeates them all, giving them order, direction, and the space to branch out deeper and deeper into knowledge.

In a way, maths is akin to the Far Eastern or Chinese calligraphy. It lies at the heart of perceived reality. And it is expressed by means of minimal symbols and numerals (like brushstrokes) applied with maximum discipline.

It's either 'right' or 'wrong'. Maths teaches you good discipline — to double-check. Unlike other subjects where there are grey areas, maths is straightforward. An answer is either right or wrong. But this 'strict' nature of maths teaches you to be disciplined, to re-examine, to learn immediately from your mistakes. And remember, you can always do better the next time. The best part of maths is that, on double-checking, you learn exactly where you went wrong.

Clear thinking shows the way. Like most other subjects, maths too must be learnt by paying attention and by concentrating. You cannot allow your mind to wander. In a literature class, if you have not been following closely, at the end you will wonder why Othello killed his wife. Maths too has its own plots. Only by understanding one part can you go on to the next. And by understanding each part, you will be able to store it away in your memory.

Clear thinking at all times is a must. When exams approach if you panic, you immediately press a mental stop button that shuts off memory and concentration. It's like a day when everything seems to go wrong — if you panic, you won't be able to do a thing. For example, if a fire breaks out and you panic, it will blaze on. But by keeping a cool mind, you will put out the fire by throwing a heavy blanket on. Or if there is a fire extinguisher close at hand, you will seize it and use. Or you will simply call the fire brigade. Similarly, while swimming, if you panic because a current is carrying you away, you won't allow your brain to tell you that by swimming diagonally you can save yourself. Or that you can try to attract the attention of a lifeguard. If he comes to your rescue and you hit out wildly or try to cling too hard, you won't be able to help him save you.

And let me tell you, even a genius cannot work if he or she is in a state of panic. If a problem seems tough, take a deep breath and address it with a cool mind-step by step and try to use your intuition. Even a hill is a mountain until you begin to climb it.

> The bear went up the mounitain
>> To see what he could see;
> And what do you think he saw?
>> The other side of the mountain...

Let us march up the mountain of maths. Once on it, we'll realise how easy it is, how it broadens our horizon. And we'll be able to see the other side of the mountain, which so far was in the shadows, out of our vision. It will enrich us individually and the human race as a whole. There's no price to pay here: just a recognition of the abilities locked within you that maths can open with its shining key.

5

Awakening the Maths Genius

We carry with us the wonders
we seek without us.
SIR THOMAS BROWNE

Since the ancient Indians gave the world mathematics, it is logical to presume that there was a great deal of mental activity in those times too. Perhaps as a means of communicating this vast knowledge, it was woven into interesting stories. Over the years, such tales came to be known collectively as Indian mythology. Unfortunately, by overemphasising the story aspect, much of the knowledge was lost as story-telling turned into pure art. Yet, you do find traces of it even today, as in the unabridged version of the *Ramayana*, which mentions an aeroplane or airship called *Pushpak*, and even goes into the details of aerodynamics.

Left side-Brain: Seat of your numerical power

The power of ancient Indian thought lies in its recognition of a lifestyle that evolved from an amalgam of science and art. The brain was perceived as the seat of power from which emanated ideas, memory, reflection, analyses, creativity, abstract forms ...

After decades of research, scientists have finally zeroed in on this mysterious, jelly-like, grey mass that resides in the skull. Our great mathematician, Nature, has blessed all of us with two 'hemispheres', or sides in the brain. In a skilful weave, she has shaped each side of the brain for specific functions.

The right side of the brain guides the left side of the body, while the left side of the brain guides the right side of the body. Why this is so is not yet understood.

The right side can be loosely labelled as the 'creative side'. It is through this section that we perceive shapes, recognise faces, remember facts. The left side or the 'doer', allows us to talk, carry out linear tasks, and guides our day-to-day activities.

The two sides, however, are not exclusive in their guiding process. They are interconnected, as neurosurgeon Dr Joseph Bogen describes, 'by a billion telephone lines.' Another researcher, psychologist Robert Ornstein has concluded that the left side guides us in our numerical abilities, while the right side enables us to recognise designs.

Developing spatial skills

The eternal optimist in me feels that it is never too late. Mathematical learning should begin at home. It's a great advantage to be able to understand and reorganise two or three-dimensional sketches visually and follow the

space-time relationship factor. It's a skill that can be acquired by anyone.

Learning to read develops an important part of the brain. Along with reading, parents ought to introduce their children to shapes and sizes, initially on flat surfaces, and later on a two or three-dimensional level.

For example:

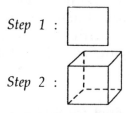

Step 1 :

Step 2 :

An anthropologist who visited an ancient tribe in Africa tried sketching three-dimensional figures for the tribes. But they were unable to comprehend them. The reason was that they had never learnt to *visualise* an object by itself, sketched on paper, as a three-dimensional figure. The part of the brain that needs to be trained had simply not been developed. It's been called *spatial visualisation* by scientists; simply put, it means being able to 'read' and restructure three-dimensional figures. I call it the 'third eye'.

To get your child started on the road to spatial visualisation, buy toys which require 'engineering' skills. The break-and-rebuild type are excellent for this purpose. So are jigsaw puzzles. Girls shouldn't be limited to dolls and tea sets. If you want your child to develop the 'third eye', toys of all kinds are a must. You must also be prepared for the complete dismemberment of the toy! It's no use nagging the child not to 'ruin' it. In the very act of dismantling and trying to put it back together, however unsuccessfully, lie the seeds of mathematics.

While taking apart a toy, the child has the opportunity to study its form. Building or rebuilding a set involves the brain in setting up a structure. Unfortunately, while boys are encouraged to play with such interesting little mind bogglers and brain builders, girls are banished to passive role playing with their dolls.

Maths in sports

Sports activities are another must for the budding mathematician. Following scores and working out averages have become an integral part of the sports scene. Whether it is tennis, football or cricket, figures are constantly flashed on the television screen and the scores or points, lengths of jumps, speeds of sprints are also buttressed with comparisons of past records. This is an excellent and entertaining way to become familiar with fractions, percentages, and ratios. Today, the child has a variety of sports to choose and learn from — with tennis players serving at 225 kmph, bowlers delivering at 150 kmph and Formula I drivers hurtling at over 210 kmph. With glitzy charts displaying world records at a glance, there is no doubt that maths has come to stay in sports. I don't mean that the child will be able to apply, say, Carl Lewis' 9.86-second sprint of 100 m in

1991, to a school maths assignment! But it certainly sends the numerals with their calculations spinning into the brain, thus laying the groundwork for interest and ability in maths.

Playing a sport is equally important. Setting a field to get the optimum result from the trajectory of the ball is a planned mathematical approach. So is allowing the body to move, twist (or even pirouette) to catch a passing ball. Such rapid reflexes are not purely physical though they may appear to be. They need quick eye movements and intuitive calculations that are all directly related to maths concepts. Such sports encompass awareness, imagery, coordination, intuition, all rolled into one flash of movement. And maths, after all, is about trajectories and velocities.

The maths alphabet

Get your child started on the road to developing the third eye with symbol games which involve simple, flat or one-dimensional figures. This will enable the child to feel comfortable and at home with symbols that are the alphabet of the maths language. To give a rough guideline, I have divided the exercise into three parts:

Symbol Analogy: Enables the child to find the numerical relationship between symbols.

Symbol Classification: Helps in classifying related symbols.

Symbol Serialisation: Guides the child in analysing the direction of a set of symbols.

Symbol analogy

1. *Question symbols:*

From the answer symbols given below, ask your child to choose the symbol that should be in place of the question mark.

Answer symbols:

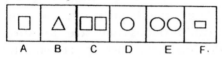

Visual steps: By examining the numerical relationship between the first two symbols, you will see that it doubles. One circle becomes two circles. So, one square becomes two squares. The answer is C.

2. *Question symbols:*

Which one should come in place of the question mark? Choose from the Answer symbols.

Answer symbols:

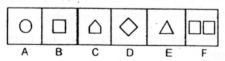

Visual steps: The first symbol has five sides, the second has one side subtracted and has four sides. So the fourth box should have one side less than the third box. The answer is E.

48

Symbol classification

1. *Question symbols:*

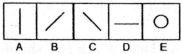

Which symbol is the odd man out?

Visual steps: The four lines A, B, C, D belong to one class. But the circle does not. So the answer is E.

2. *Question symbols:*

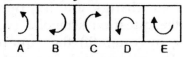

Which symbol is the odd man out?

Visual steps: A, C, D, E are pointing horizontally up or down. But only one is pointing vertically down. So the odd man out is B.

Symbol serialisation

1. *Question symbols:*

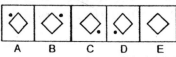

Where should the dot be on E? Choose from the Answer symbols.

Answer symbols:

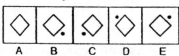

Visual steps: The dot moves in a clockwise direction. So the answer is D.

2. *Question symbols:*

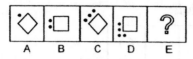

From the Answer symbols, which one should be
in E?

Answer symbols:

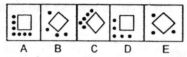

Visual steps: Two things are happening
simultaneously in the question symbols: (i) the
dots are increasing by one, (ii) the square is
changing direction. The answer is C since it fulfils
both requirements.

By such ingenious methods, you and your
child will develop the third eye. Most of you have
a 'Family Hour' when you play cards or word
games. So why not include these 'symbol games'
too?

Later, you can move on to three-dimensional
symbol games, such as *Turn the Box*, which goes
this way:

Question box:

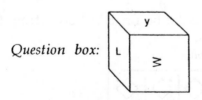

Which box from the Answer boxes is the same
as the one above?

50

Answer boxes:

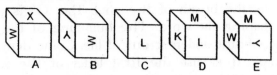

Visual steps: While you can reason out the answer, the right way to do it is to fix the image of the first box in your mind. Now, mentally rotate the image. When it clicks into place, you will have found the right box, which is E.

Please remember, these are only simple mind games. If you or your child find them too difficult, don't despair. It shouldn't stop you from taking higher maths. While I would like you to develop your third eye to its fullest potential, I wouldn't want you to be put off the subject because you experienced a bit of difficulty. Remember, even in the mathematical world there are many fallacies. It could well be that 'spatial' visualisation is not an all-important factor in the learning of maths. Look at it this way — even the best writer in the world needn't be a perfect speller to love words, live words, and feel a sense of fulfilment as he writes.

That is exactly what I am doing. By introducing the world of symbols to you, I am making you and your child as comfortable with them as a writer is with words.

Take the word *Om*. Hindus believe it is the essence, the breath of the soul. The 'O' is your lips shaping the word. The humming of the 'M' is the vibrant undercurrent of life. Coincidentally, perhaps, it is also the first letter of the word 'Maths'. Make maths a part of your life. After all, it is the vibration that moves the entire world!

6

Nurturing Mathability

He who would learn to fly one day must first learn to stand and walk and run and climb and dance; one cannot fly into flying.

FRIEDRICH NIETZSCHE

Call it love at first sight or what you will, but when I was only three years old I fell in love with numbers. It was as if nothing else existed as I worked out sums. Everything else faded into oblivion as I got the right answers. I found a companionship that gave me a deep sense of emotional security and fulfilment. Perhaps I was too young to understand why this was so.

Now that I'm older and wiser, I can look back and understand what numbers meant to me. They were the rock that gave me strength. They were the numerous little soldiers that stood and defended me fearlessly. They were the pillars of my life. With numbers I knew I was safe, because no matter how the world changed, no matter what I heard or saw, I knew one unchanging force in my life would always be there: numbers that gave me a beautiful message of hope — that two plus two *always* made four.

All of us need this constant factor in our lives. What bliss it is to feel that, come hell or high water, this factor never changes. It's the strong thread in our lives. It keeps us whole when other things could be shredding or falling to pieces around us.

The unbreakable thread

I want to share the magic of numbers with you because I have experienced what they can do. Friends may come and go, but numbers remain with you eternally. They are not just the symbols written in chalk on the blackboard. If you allow them to, they will spring out and join you. They will guide you into an adventurous world and thrill you with their variety and applications. They have a wide range that can never be encompassed. They have a richness that you'd never dreamed of. Together with their many faces and phases, they have that one important quality that we look for in our friends, lovers, families — the constant factor.

Stability in an unstable world — that is what maths is all about. That is why I say maths is the pulse of our lives; the thread that keeps us together; the thread that never breaks.

Psychologists have harnessed this factor to bring solace to all the troubled minds that land on their couches. When a person is unhappy, he is told to make a list of what makes him sad.

He should also make a list of what he is blessed with. On this mathematical equation hangs the balance of pessimism and optimism.

I know a woman who has been paralysed for the past 20 years. Yet, she is always cheerful, always smiling, always interested in everything. When I asked her how she kept her spirits up, she replied, 'Whenever I feel low, I make a list of all that I have to be thankful for. That list includes loving, caring children, enough money to live on comfortably, a lovely home, and the greatest blessing of all — to be alive to enjoy the beautiful world around me.'

Because she is paralysed, she is unable to do many of the things that others can. 'One day, I asked myself why I exist if I can't do so many things,' she continued. 'I thought for a long time. I know we are all here for a specific purpose. So what was mine? And the answer came to me: I was here to make others happy! And the only way I can make others happy is by being cheerful myself.'

Indeed, she has found the magic of a mathematical equation. It is:

Awareness + Cheerfulness = Happiness

or

$$A + C = H$$

Enumerating thoughts

Psychologists or psychiatrists ask us to make lists. In other words, they are asking us to *enumerate* our thoughts. By breaking down emotions into

55

simple arithmetic, we often find the solutions. That is why the woman I have spoken about makes a list of what she is blessed with. We make shopping lists so that we remember what we need to make our lives comfortable. We make a list of the pros and cons before taking an important decision. For example, if you are offered a new job, you write down certain points:

Old Job	
Pros	*Cons*
1. Known, trusted colleagues	1. Lower salary
2. Confirmed job	2. Same rut
	3. Family business, so no chance of accelerated promotion
	4. No travel
	5. No provident fund
	6. No perks

New Job	
Pros	*Cons*
1. Better salary	1. New faces
2. New challenge	2. Probation period
3. Chances of faster promotion	
4. Travel abroad	
5. Provident fund	
6. Perks	

Such a list instantly gives you the total picture. It also helps you to understand what is troubling you. Perhaps you can talk it over with your new boss, pointing out that with your wide experience, you needn't be put on probation.

Lists clean out the mind and make clear thinking possible. If a problem confronts you, the best way to deal with it is to write it down, breaking it into clear, demarcated segments. The sheer philosophy and the inbuilt nature of maths come to your aid, and offers you either a solution or the path to a solution.

Why are such lists made? They have therapeutic value. Decisions cannot be made when your mind is clouded by emotions and confused thoughts. Maths is the ray of sunshine that dispels those clouds and shows you the clear, blue sky that was always there beneath the misty curtain in your mind.

Perhaps that is why maths is seen as a cold, clinical, calculating science. But that's putting a quality to its face. It's like calling a surgeon cruel because he wields a scalpel on the operating table. Yet maths, like the surgeon, has a helpful, caring persona that shows you the light at the end of a long, dark tunnel.

When you are angry, you count under your breath: '1–2–3–4–5...' until you calm down. When you are unable to sleep, you count sheep. When you are depressed, you confide in your friend and feel better because, by sharing your worries, you have *halved* them.

What does it all mean? What does it all boil down to? That *maths is the science of an art — the art of living*. Maths is inherent in your lifestyle. Maths is the obliging friend who shows you the way. It is only your *emotions* that have blocked you from seeing what maths is. It is the constant factor that brings stability to your life. It liberates you from problems. It is a constant companion in your evolution.

Equations of attitude

How does maths work for you? For a start, you must accept that it is always there for you to lean on — the constant factor, the rock. Next, suppose you have a dream or a wish, how do you make it come true? If you do not apply a *positive mathematical equation* to it, it won't come true. Here is how you do it in simple arithmetic:

$$\text{Dream} + \text{Action} = \text{Reality}$$

Maths tells you that the next step to a dream is to act. The end result is the dream turning into reality. Maths gives you the channel, the viaduct, the infrastructure to realise your dream.

You can further divide the first equation by setting goals to reach that reality.

Goal as in:

G: Go for it!

O: Over and above if required.

A: Another way if a dead end is reached.

L: Licked into shape!

In arithmetical terms, it would read as:

$$1$$
$$+1$$
$$+1$$
$$+1$$
$$\overline{= 4}$$

$$\text{or} \quad 1 \times 4 = 4$$

What has maths done? It has been with you at every step of the way. It has helped you make a list. It has by its very equation, liberated your dreams. It has created a strong structure for you to build upon. It has made your way easier by further subdividing. It has helped you reach your dreamed-of destination. It has made a reality of what you may have thought was impossible.

When you have been ridden with anxiety in the process of reaching your goal, it has kept the picture in front of you. It has held on to that goal even while you were awash with emotion. It has given you that gentle push when you needed it because it refused to join those clouds in your mind. All along, it has moved you on steadily to the next goalpost. In short, it has always been there. And most importantly, it has never let you down.

Maths within

The best part is that maths is not an outsider. It is within you, in your every heartbeat, in your brain. You have within you the maths-factor that has made you go on. It is the rock or the spine that held steadfast while another part of you gave in.

Those who say, 'I'm poor at maths,' are doing themselves an injustice. They are only undermining themselves when they need not. It's like saying, 'I'm poverty-stricken,' when a range of riches glitters before you.

Those who say, 'Numbers scare me,' should think again. Numbers have brought them to where they are. They are the soldiers of the borders of the mind, guarding it in times of difficulties. They don't use guns or ammunition, but something stronger and more long-lasting — faith.

Those who say, 'I don't have the patience to do maths,' are mistaken. They view maths as an imposition on their time. It is not. It brings organisation into your life. And it is because of this organisation that you can go ahead — perhaps to bigger things.

So if you have a goal, don't let your emotions rule you and convince you otherwise. Miracles happen because you have worked towards them systematically. An artist shows you a finished, glowing canvas. He has worked on it with precision, with a structure. So should you. Hold on to the constant factor within you and allow it to liberate your dreams. Give yourself a chance by letting your maths-factor work for you. Make maths the pillar of your life!

7

Language of Maths

*D*o you realise that every time you say, 'I don't have a mathematical mind,' you are insulting your own intelligence? Let me explain why.

Maths is a way of thinking. Its language is based on numbers and symbols. Animals, our four-footed friends, have a hazy concept of maths. Human beings, with their superior mental abilities, have developed this concept into practical science.

You may wonder how I can make the bold assumption that animals have some idea of maths. I will illustrate this with an incident I once witnessed.

A friend of mine has a beautiful Labrador bitch called Judy. One day, Judy delivered several adorable little pups. She licked each one and appeared to be very proud of her progeny. Since there were too many pups for my friend to handle, she started giving them away. Judy was not around when her first pup was carried off by the new owner. Later, when she went to the basket for her daily loving lick, she paused, then she turned to my friend and gave a little whine. You see, Judy knew instinctively that one pup was missing! Obviously she had never been to school or been taught maths. But she knew the difference between *six* pups and *seven* pups.

Judy's *concept* of maths was guided by instinct. Human beings have it too, but we have gone a few steps further. Our sophisticated brains have evolved it *and given concrete shape to a way of thinking that is already within us.* We have given it labels in the form of numbers. Where Judy may realise a pup is missing, we would say *one* pup is missing. We would also know that a pup here and a pup there make it *two* pups. Thus, we put it down mathematically as:

$$1 + 1 = 2$$

How easy it is for us today to say 'plus' or 'minus'! The two symbols (+ and −) came into being in the fifteenth century. If a box of goods weighed more than it should, the merchants marked it as '+'. This symbol was derived from the Latin word 'et', which means 'and', as it still does in French.

When a box weighed less than it should, the merchant marked it as '−'. It is possible that the minus sign derived from the plus sign. Thus, minus could have been | or −, since a combination of the two gave +. Since | could have been confused with the number one, the merchant settled for the horizontal −.

That brings me to the equal (=) symbol. In 1557, mathematician Robert Recorde realised that two parallel lines of the same length were 'equal'. Thus, he wrote it down as =.

Coming back to Judy, her species has not been able to evolve the maths-concept into a science as we have. But the fact remains that she has a vague idea of maths. So, can you honestly say to yourself, 'I don't have a mathematical mind'? The simple truth is that each one of us possesses a mathematical mind. Today, even an illiterate person can say, 'I have *three* children.'

The Maths Alphabet

Numbers and symbols are the alphabet of maths. The methods of adding, subtracting, multiplying, dividing are akin to word-building in a language. And the problems are like the sentences or paragraphs of a language. Numbers and symbols may put you off maths, but consider this: a shorthand stenographer uses *symbols* to take dictation; a blind person, by feel, reads Braille through dot formations which, indeed, are symbols; even our language, or rather the act of writing it, has symbols. We have:

. to denote a full stop.

, to denote a pause.

! to denote exclamation.

? to denote a question.

We read them every day, and they have become a part of our thinking. If we didn't have these symbols, we wouldn't be able to write sentences. We wouldn't be able to communicate. And maths *is* communication.

In language, we have writers who have evolved words. Largely, our languages today are derived from Latin or Sanskrit. Then we have the regional dialects.

Similarly in maths, we have mathematicians who have evolved the maths language, and the maths we learn today is a derivation or a progression. The only difference is that in maths we don't have dialects — except perhaps at a limited level. For example, as mentioned in Chapter 3, what in India is referred to as 'one *lakh*' is known as 'one hundred thousand' in the West. But these are mere labels. In the maths language, both a *lakh* and one hundred thousand would be written with the number one followed by five zeros, with a slight variation in the placement of the commas:

India   : 1,00,000

UK/US : 100,000

This is why a rich man in India is called a *lakhpati*. In the West, he is a 'millionaire'. These are labels derived from a single and easy word. After all, it would be quite a mouthful to say: 'hundred thousandaire'!

In the English language, we have had several great writers and poets, such as Charles Dickens, Jane Austen, William Shakespeare, to name a few, who clothed their ideas — based on their experiences — in beautiful words and sentences to convey their meaning to the reader.

Similarly, maths has its great luminaries such as Pascal, Descartes, Eratosthenes. They too dressed their ideas, based on their experiences and experiments, in numerals and problems to convey their message to the reader. But, before I go on to quoting a passage from the works of one of these great masters, I'd like to give you a simple, comparative analysis between language and maths.

In a language, the alphabet is divided into vowels and consonants, as:

Vowels   : *a, e, i, o, u*

Consonants: *b, c, d, f, g, h,* and
    on through to *z*

Similarly in maths, you have numbers. They are divided into prime numbers and composite numbers, as:

Prime numbers   : 2, 3, 5, 7, 11, 13
Composite numbers: 9, 15, 25, 32,
                              and so on

As you will see, prime numbers are an entity in themselves. They cannot be divided. You cannot divide 2, 3, 5, 7, 11 and 13 by any number.

Composite numbers are divisible. For example:

$$\frac{9}{3} = 3$$

$$\frac{15}{3} = 5 \quad \text{or} \quad \frac{15}{5} = 3$$

$$\frac{25}{5} = 5$$

$$\frac{32}{2} = 16, \text{ and so on.}$$

In school, we are taught this with words such as 'integer', 'factors', etc. I have deliberately kept it simple to make for better understanding.

Eratosthenes' sieve

Now that you have grasped the 'vowels' and 'consonants' of maths, you will enjoy the passage I am about to quote from one of the great masters of mathematics.

About twenty-two centuries ago, there was a Greek geographer and astronomer called Eratosthenes. He invented a sieve to sift and filter the prime numbers from the composite numbers. It was a beautiful piece of art. He wrote the composite numbers in six columns. He circled the primes, crossing out all multiples of 2 by a clever stroke of his pen. Similarly, he circled the number 3 and crossed out all multiples of 3, and so also the multiples of 5 and 7. Finally, the remaining circled numbers were the primes.

Just as Dickens formulated sentences in the English language, Eratosthenes formulated mathematical sentences. Dickens dazzled us with his evocative prose, Eratosthenes dazzled us with his evocative mathematical prose.

I do agree that you may find that reading Eratosthenes' passage is not the same as reading a passage by Dickens. Here I'd appeal to you to call upon that aesthetic sense you are blessed with and use it the way you would to 'read' or view a Picasso painting. You'd admire the artist's clean brush strokes. So can you admire the fine, clean lines of Eratosthenes' sieve. I am sure a maths 'literary critic' would write about it this way:

> In a revolutionary, trailblazing method, the geographer and astronomer, Eratosthenes, has tapped the essence of mathematics. He has captured the inherent dynamics of maths with his pen. The clarity with which it has been set down will motivate maths fans to venture into areas never before explored.
>
> With this unique sieve, Eratosthenes lays down a clear, shining, positive approach. With one glance, maths aficionados can now find practical, creative solutions to

problems. By inventing the wheel of mathematics, Eratosthenes has abolished the need to reinvent it at every stage for every problem.

Now read Eratosthenes' sieve:

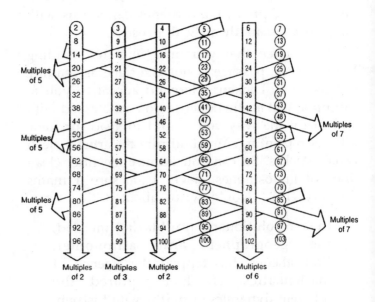

If you have gone through the sieve and digested the tiniest morsel from it, it means that you have understood the spirit of this chapter. Earlier, you might have looked at Eratosthenes' sieve simply as a box of numerals with arrows crisscrossing it, just flipped the page over or even closed the book. If you had, remember, it would not have been because you *don't* possess a mathematical brain but because *that* part of your brain was not stimulated enough, not for the lack of ability, but for the lack of interest. It is not that you lacked potential, but that you were living *below* your potential.

The fourth dimension

My idea is to show you that you have within you a greater energy, a greater creativity, a greater problem-solving capacity than you give yourself credit for. You have the third eye but have not used it so far. You have viewed the world three-dimensionally. As you read this book, I want you to feel the fourth dimension within you.

You may wonder how opening your third eye would give you a fourth dimension? Sounds illogical, doesn't it? But you will understand what I mean when I tell you that the two eyes you possess show you a three-dimensional world. This point was brought home when a relative had an accident. He had to have one eye bandaged. He could see clearly with his good eye, but when I unthinkingly held out a photograph which I wanted him to see, in the act of taking it from me, he missed it by a few inches.

Similarly, I feel that by keeping the third eye closed, you miss grasping maths by a few inches. All you have to do is open the third eye!

8

Mastering Mathability

They can because they think they can.
VIRGIL

I have said over and over again, in different ways, that each one possesses a mathematical brain. We have the seeds of maths, the ingrained power of understanding the subject, deep within us. Now another question arises. How do we draw out that power so that we can drive away that feeling of alienness, and use it to its fullest potential? How do we turn ourselves from maths aliens into maths lovers?

I always had the answers in my mind but did not have the right words to express them. One day, however, while reading the newspaper, my eye fell on a beautiful line in an advertisement. It read: 'Magic of drip irrigation — turning deserts into goldmines'. In a flash, I had found the words! I knew now how I should convey those answers! Paragraphs formed in my mind, words jostled and collided with thoughts.

Mental Drip Irrigation: The four Cs

If I liken that part of the brain that lies unused due to maths alienness to a desert, then the cure lies in mental drip irrigation! I want your brain to soak and absorb the water of knowledge. I will give it to you, drop by drop.

To irrigate the desert and turn it into a maths goldmine, you need only four drops of water. Let each one drip into you, and your thirsty brain will open its folds to drink it. What are those four drops of water?

They are the four Cs:

Common sense

Confidence

Concentration

Control

Surprised? But that is all you need to turn yourself into a mathematician! I will take each drop on my finger so that you can see it shimmering and illuminating your inner mind, thus opening your third eye.

Common sense: Every maths problem needs a good strong dose of this special drop. It tells you that nothing is beyond your ken. If a problem is set before you, read it carefully. Remember, it need not freeze your mind into a state of panic. It is a problem that has a solution. All you have to do is apply your common sense to it.

To help you draw on this drop, let me ask you a mathematical question:

> If 6 men can pack 6 packets of candy in 6 minutes, how many men are required to pack 60 packets in 60 minutes?

Read it carefully. Now apply your common sense. The first thing that should strike you is that you do not necessarily need more men. Why? Because you have more time to pack that candy!

Now write it step by step:

1. 6 men pack 6 boxes in 6 minutes
2. 6 men pack 1 box in 1 minute
3. 6 men pack 60 boxes in 60 minutes.

Painless, wasn't it? To the maths-alien, however, it appears to be a complex problem. She reads it, feels that it is too difficult and clams up mentally. Also, the robotic manner of teaching maths in school doesn't help, and the clever way in which the problem has been worded makes you focus on the number of men immediately. But a little thinking irrigated by common sense, will show you that this is not so.

If it had been worded in another way, you would have found it simpler:

> If 6 men can pack 6 packets of candy in 6 minutes, how many packets of candy would they pack in 60 minutes?

Knowing that the number of men remains constant, you'd write:

1. In 6 minutes, 6 packets are packed.
2. In 1 minute, 1 packet is packed.
3. In 60 minutes, 60 packets are packed.

But the way it was worded the first time calls for that one drop of common sense! So you see, it is as easy as eating candy!

Confidence. Another drop required to tackle a maths problem is confidence. The great confidence of a bulldozer. Plough into a problem with the firm, strong feeling in you that you can do it. Nobody, not even yourself, will dare to question you!

I notice that many people feel there is a 'trick' to solving a maths problem. When someone shows you how to solve a seemingly complex problem, the human ego comes into play. She makes it appear so easy, you want to crawl into a corner to hide yourself. You wonder why she found it so easy, and you didn't? What your 'tricky' problem-solver has conveniently forgotten to tell you is that she had come across it earlier than you and had taken the time to get a grasp of it, or that she may have stumbled on to it by accident. She leaves out these tiny details and makes you feel like a 'dumbo'.

While the 'tricky' problem-solver may appear to be handing you a method on a silver platter, be wary. In the long run, her method may not work. It will not work if you have merely adapted it but not understood it. It will not work even for her, because she sees it as a clever trick or short cut. Which means that for each problem she has to find a new 'trick'.

The best way to learn maths is to allow your natural intelligence to take over. With a clear, confident mind, you will be able to do it.

Concentration. Every Indian, when confronted with the drop of concentration, will instantly think of Prince Arjuna in the *Mahabharata.* It is an oft-repeated tale, but I must narrate it here to underline the importance of concentration.

Dronacharya taught archery to the royal princes of Hastinapura. One day, he decided to test their power of concentration. Gathering his royal pupils around him, he pointed to the target — a bird on the branch of a tree. They had to shoot the bird and bring it down. The first candidate for the concentration test was Prince Yudhisthira.

'What do you see?' asked Drona, as the prince readied himself with the bow and arrow.

'I see the bird, the branch on which it sits, and the leaves of the tree,' replied the prince.

'What else?' demanded Drona.

'The tree, the sky, you — my teacher — and my brothers,' said Yudhisthira.

Drona called the other princes — Duryodhana and Bhima. They gave the same reply. Poor Drona was saddened. He felt he had failed as a teacher.

Finally, with a heavy heart, he called Prince Arjuna.

'Do you see the bird?' he asked hopelessly.

'I do,' replied the prince, confidently.

'What else do you see?' asked Drona.

'I see only the bird,' replied Prince Arjuna steadfastly.

'Do you not see the tree, the sky, myself — your teacher — and beyond?' queried Drona, hope lifting his heart.

'I see only the bird,' repeated Arjuna stubbornly.

'What part of the bird do you see?'

'Only the eye!' said Arjuna.

This was the answer Drona had hoped for. It displayed Prince Arjuna's power of concentration.

What does concentration do? It helps you to focus. It blocks out anxiety and emotions. If a sportsman were to worry about being tackled by his opponents as he runs for the goal, he would never get started. Think of maths as a fun-sport. Your goal is to get at the solution, to net it.

The point I am making is that when a maths problem is presented to a person, she allows her anxiety to take over. *She creates those exceptional circumstances in her mind*. Instead, if the emotions were blocked out by concentrating, he or she would set out calmly to understand the nature of the maths problem and work on a method to solve it.

The best way to concentrate is to switch to neutral gear. Don't think in terms of 'Oh God, how will I do it?' or 'What if I cannot do it?' Be aware that though you are a highly intelligent person, it is *not* your intelligence that is on trial. Read each sentence with concentration. For example, if the problem is written thus:

A woman spends Rs 230.50 on an average during the first 8 months. During the next 4 months, she spends Rs 180 on an average. During that year, she takes a loan of Rs 164. What is her average monthly income of that year?

First, read the problem carefully. Next, enumerate data. Then allow your common sense and confidence to tell you that you can do it.

Concentrate on the problem, and begin by outlining the data in simple steps. Instantly, you have the answer:

1. Sum of money she spends in 8 months

   $8 \times 230.50 = 1844$

2. Sum of money she spends in the next 4 months

   $4 \times 180 = 720$

3. Total money spent in 12 months

$$1844 + 720 = 2564$$

4. Loan taken is not part of her income. Therefore,

$$2564 - 164 = 2400$$

5. Thus her monthly income

$$\frac{2400}{12} = Rs\ 200$$

Why is concentration so important? *It acts as a catalyst towards defusing the I-can't-do-it feeling.* Negative thoughts make you focus on the irrelevant. Instead, if you bring your powers of concentration to bear on the maths problem, you shift your focus to what is relevant.

Sometimes, words and numbers defeat you at the first reading. But if you don't allow such defeatist thoughts to creep in, you are already on the right path. Confidence in yourself will drive you to focus on the right clue. It will enable you to see the problem in simple terms. This keeps the feeling of frustration and the sense of defeat at bay.

Decimals might be another reason for you to feel discouraged. You feel that if you were given round figures, you would be able to solve the maths problem easily. Fine. Think along those lines.

Suppose the woman spends Rs 200 (instead of 230.50) in the first 8 months, how would you tackle it? You would multiply 200 by 8. Write that down. Now apply the same method to the actual problem. So you will write it now as 230.50×8.

Simplifying a problem makes you understand it better. With understanding comes the feeling that it is manageable. You can simplify it if you concentrate on it.

Control. The first three Cs — Common sense, Confidence and Concentration — add up to the fourth C — Control. Once you have doused anxiety, fear, panic with those three precious drops, you will automatically feel in control of the situation. But you must *feel* you are in control. You must *tell* yourself that you are in control.

Look on maths as a purring sports car. You are the driver. You are at the helm. There's no way you are going to relinquish the wheel to another. If you are driving uphill, you will drive slowly. Similarly in maths, take your time. Understand each number and symbol. Analyse what is required. You, the controller, have three strings attached to your fingertips — the data, the method, the solution. As you take each step, or go into the next gear, you will find it gets easier.

How do you always ensure that you are in control? If you find that despite taking the step-by-step approach, you have reached a dead end, don't give up. Go to an easier problem. An easy problem gives you that sense of control because you know you can solve it. Often, a shift in gears will give you a fresh perspective on how to solve the more complex problem.

I know a writer of short stories who decided to try her hand at writing a novel. After a few months of intense scribbling, she found she couldn't go on. As she told me, 'I felt I had lost control of the characters, the plot. I didn't know in which direction my story was heading.' What did she do? Did she give up writing altogether? Not at all. She put the novel aside and went back to writing short stories. She regained control. She then approached the novel with the same sense of being at the helm. She took up the book, chapter by chapter, and within six months, she had finished her book!

The sense of control is important not only in your approach to maths, but to everything in life. If you let the four Cs, the four life-giving drops irrigate your mind, you will never regret it. Your mind will bloom with the knowledge given by these drops. And you will find that it is not only maths that you wish to explore, but other areas as well! After all, life is an eternal voyage of self-discovery.

9

Mathability: Problem Solving

*It isn't that they can't see the solution,
it's that they can't see the problem.*

G.K. CHESTERTON

*E*ach one of us is blessed with that intangible ability called intuition. It is a mother's intuition that tells her why the baby is crying. When your car suddenly starts making strange knocking sounds, it is the mechanic's intuition that tells him what has come loose. When there is a power failure, it is the electrician's intuition that tells him what could be wrong and where he should start.

Solving maths problems too requires intuition. My statement may come as a surprise to you. All this time you thought that maths was a matter of memorising formulae, using a logical, step-by-step approach, and that was it.

Mathematical mind games

But think about it. What exactly is intuition? What is that special flash that illuminates a problem and shows you the way? Is it a gift from God? It is — like everything else. Intuition is *seeing relationships based on personal experiences.*

For example, how would you solve this problem:

> If 5 tyres were used on a car which has travelled 20,000 miles, how many miles would each tyre sustain, if all the tyres were used equally in sustaining this mileage?

If you approach this problem purely 'logically' without seeing relationships, you would simply divide 20,000 by 5 and come up with the answer: 4000 miles. How did you arrive at this answer? By a simple formula of division. But you got the wrong answer!

Here is where your experience and the ability to work out relationships come in handy. For example, you might wonder if the car in this problem runs on five tyres instead of the normal four!

The intuitive person, however, will work it out in this way, to arrive at the right answer:

— When the car travels one mile, each of the 4 tyres sustains one mile's use.

— So when a car travels 20,000 miles, a total of (20,000 × 4) 80,000 tyre miles are used.

— Since the mileage has been gathered on 5 tyres, each tyre has used

$$\frac{80,000}{5} = 16,000 \text{ miles.}$$

Another intuitive person may solve the problem this way:

Since 4 out of 5 tyres are being used:

$$\frac{4}{5} \times 20,000 = 16,000 \text{ miles.}$$

What did you deduce from this exercise? If your answer was 4000 miles, don't be disheartened. At the first reading, you were probably relieved that it was a simple matter of division. Without stopping to think, you rushed into that formula, thinking: 'Ah, for once, I've got it!' Had you stopped to analyse it, I am sure you would have realised it was wrong.

Your instant response is the human factor I have talked about all along. The image of maths that is so prevalent, is that it is a mechanical process.

Using your imagination

If we had been taught from an early age that maths is a living, vibrant science, I am sure we would have seen it in its totality. And in viewing it as a larger practical science, we would have collectively developed the maths intuition.

As it stands, in class or at home, children are made to do maths in an automatic, unimaginative way. With the idea fixed in their brains that 'the teacher's method is the right one', students do not develop their own thinking. Or even realise that it is possible to do so. Very rarely are they encouraged to work out their own methods. Thus, while they add, subtract, multiply, divide, they do it mechanically, like a calculator rather than as thinking persons.

Since this happens to many people, those who display more thinking powers, more imagination, more intuition, are seen as having a 'mathematical mind'. What appears to be a complex problem to Sheila is child's play to Rajiv. The fact is that the quality of exposure to maths differs between these two people. As a result, Rajiv makes *connections*. He sees the links or relationships in problems that Sheila does not.

What adults fail to teach children is that a formula is purely a means to solving a problem. It is not the be-all and end-all of maths. For example, Arun, a geology student, tells me about a new problem he was given in school:

> If 2 men can build a 10-feet high wall in 20 days, how long will 5 men take to build the same wall?

Arun says: 'I remember this vividly because I was the only student to get the right answer. Even the ones we saw as the "brains" of maths rushed to answer, 50 days! At home, we had some construction work going on. I remember my father telling the contractor to put more men on the job to get the work done faster. So I worked it out the other way and figured the answer was 8 days.'

As you can see, Arun's personal experience came in handy in maths. He was able to link the fact that more men would take less time to do the same job. In this common-sense factor lie the seeds of what is mathematically called inverse proportion. Unfortunately, students are not always taught a formula from a common-sense approach. The result: they memorise the formula and are then unable to use it or apply it when different problems arise.

Conceptualising problems

Intuition is all about *understanding through experience*. Haven't you often said: 'If I had known this in school, I would have understood it better?' Now that you have experienced that something, you are able to apply it to the theory you were taught in school. What you are now experiencing is that special flash of insight which has risen from your intuition working on the wheels of your experience.

In the practice of medicine, an experienced doctor intuitively knows what could be wrong with a patient. Based on this and his examination,

84

he tells the patient to carry out specific tests. A less experienced doctor might not get this flash of intuition and may have to ask for a wider range of tests to be carried out. Similarly, a 'maths-doctor' practises maths based on his own experience.

This is interesting, because it means you are never too old to learn maths. Unlike a student, an adult's approach to maths is experience. And that is certainly a plus point! In fact, I see life as an eternal learning process. Regardless of age, we are all students. People who say, 'I'm too old to learn,' are only demeaning their maturity.

An adult knows that his fixed deposit amount in the bank yields, say, 11 per cent. Here, he experiences for himself the theory of percentages that he had learnt in school. But in school, he had absorbed the method of percentages purely as an abstract mathematical formula. As I have said earlier, intuition arises out of the quality of exposure to maths.

Start with simple problems. Then go on to more complex ones. Collect bits and pieces of information and punch them into your memory. Then, whenever you come across a problem, you can sort through your 'knowledge-bank', using your experience and common sense creatively to solve it.

The right solution is there in the brain, but maths-aliens do not give themselves enough time to think and thus perceive the solution.

The very act of perceiving an idea, the thinking process, is called *conceptualisation*. It is the vital key to problem-solving. It is a mental lever. You weigh one idea. If it does not work, you try another. The greater the choice of concepts that you give yourself, the greater the chances of your solving a problem.

Overcoming mental blocks

Quite often, however, a person comes up against a mental or conceptual block. The reason could be panic, a negative approach, a clue read incorrectly, or the wrong focus. Problem-setters use this human factor and exploit it to lead you into what appears to be a daunting maze. Actually, the problem-setter is giving you an opportunity to use your intelligence, your analytical powers.

To solve a problem you may have to use a familiar process in a new way, you may have to abandon a conventional idea, you may even have to reassemble certain components to make a new arrangement . . . . The rugby player's approach does not work, though it looks tempting enough. It brings you back to square one. Whereas, if you think for five minutes longer and work at it systematically, chances are you will be closer to reaching your goal in less time.

If you feel you still have a mental block, form an image in your mind. Suppose you were confronted with a high wall. What would you do? Would you beat your head against it? No. Would you walk away from it? No. You would try to find a way to walk around it or climb over it.

Similarly, in maths, try to walk *around* the mental block. By opening your mind to a new approach, you will be engaging in a creative process. You will be taking a subconscious leap. A *leap*, not a mere step. It is a geometrical, not an arithmetical progression. You have taken this leap after a good deal of thought, after much stirring in your brain, after a host of ideas have whirled, shifted, collided, and finally emerged as a pattern. That is when you experience that special flash — intuition!

The hungry dogs!

Let me animate it for you. You have two dogs called Rambo and Hammer. You have tied both of them on one short leash.

Diagram 1

The diagram above shows that Rambo and Hammer are at the centre of the line C. On either side you have placed a large bowl of dog food — A is one bowl and B is the other. The two dogs are hungry. What do they do? Rambo tries to reach A, while Hammer tries to reach B. Thus:

Diagram 2

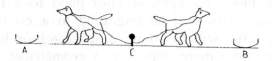

Neither can reach its respective bowl. The leash is too short. They try again, harder:

Diagram 3

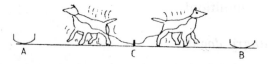

No luck. Hungry, they sit down at C once again, and look at each other nonplussed:

Diagram 4

They have to think of a new way to appease their hunger. Finally, both turn to bowl A and eat:

Diagram 5

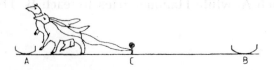

Then both turn to the bowl B to eat:

Diagram 6

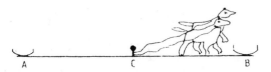

By trying, thinking, analysing, Rambo and Hammer had a flash of intuition which they carried out in Diagrams 5 and 6!

So you see, intuition is embedded in each one of us. Sometimes, or more often than not, it arises from a practical situation and collides with maths which is seen as an abstract science. Knowledge and intuition are intertwined in a constant cyclic motion. What you should do is hook on to it and the world of maths will open out to you in one big, glorious, grand flash of intuition!

You can do it!

10

Logic of Mathability

Nothing is particularly hard if you divide it into small jobs.

HENRY FORD

*D*o you know something? I envy you. You are on the verge of a discovery. Looking at maths again with fresh eyes is rather like going out on your first date. It has all the breathless excitement that goes with it. The introductions have been made. The spark has been lit. Now, it's a progression.

The best part about relearning maths is its uncanny resemblance to a first date, where you hang on to each other's words. You talk about your likes and dislikes. You discover the things you have in common. In other words, you talk about yourself as you are. Then, an interested query from your date leads you back to your childhood, and back again to the present. Perhaps you touch on the future.

That is what learning or relearning maths in adulthood is all about. You bring to it your experience, and start somewhere in the 'middle', with a feeling of exhilaration because you don't have to start again, from the beginning. Somewhere along the way, you call on what you have learnt in the past. And you realise that the grounding makes sense to you now after all these years!

Most people sail through adding, subtracting, multiplying, and dividing. They take to fractions like a fish to water. They dive into the sea of numbers, flick their fins and pick out simple fractions. It is wonderful to know, for example, that half of a pie is written as $\frac{1}{2}$. And that it denominates one part of an entire piece. The number above the line is the 'part' and is called the numerator, while the number below the line is the 'whole' and is called the denominator.

Mastering the methods

The beauty of the language of maths lies in its short, precise terms. If you were to put it into words, you would be writing long essays that would only confuse you! In its essence, the maths language saves you both time and energy. As you master it and its methods you can, within minutes, arrive at your answer.

Every fraction has a wealth of meaning to it. For example, $\frac{1}{2}$ can mean:

a. *Sharing:*

One half of a whole pie.

b. *Computing:*

One amongst others. For example, you can say 'one out of two children born every day has brown eyes.'

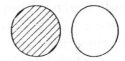

c. *Comparisons:*

One compared to another (ratio).

d. *Mathematical:*

One divided by two.

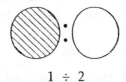

$$1 \div 2$$

It is all so simple. Where is the barrier? After talking to several people, I discovered that the confusion begins when they first learn fractions, decimals, and percentages.

The problem in understanding, as I see it, arises when a child is taught addition, subtraction, multiplication, and division as independent segments. So the mind is set on that course. Every new segment that is taught thereafter is seen as independent in itself.

Yet, fractions, decimals, and percentages converge, unlike the first four segments. For example, you cannot change adding into subtracting. Yet, you are asked to change fractions into decimals or percentages. It looks difficult, because in your mind, fractions, decimals, and percentages should stand apart from one another.

What many fail to understand is that fractions, decimals, and percentages are the *same* segment, but *expressed* in a different way. They are *translations* of each other, not *transformations*. They are another way of understanding and expressing the same thing.

In the English language, you can express the word *possible* as *conceivable* or *probable*, depending on the context. Similarly, in maths, fractions, decimals or percentages are used, *depending on the context*. The differences are slight, but important.

In decimals, the denominator is always in tens. For example, you can write a fraction as $\frac{1}{2}$, $\frac{1}{4}$, $\frac{7}{6}$, You cannot do this with decimals. Here, tens, hundreds, thousands, etc., are always the whole or the denominator. For example:

Decimal   Fraction

$$0.1 = \frac{1}{10}$$

$$0.01 = \frac{1}{100}$$

93

$$0.001 = \frac{1}{1000}.$$

Percentage is a specialised department of fractions and decimals. Here, the denominator is always 100:

Percentage	Fraction	Decimal
4%	$\frac{4}{100}$ or $\frac{1}{25}$	0.04

The scaffolding element

So far, so good. But what a mathematician like me takes for granted is not as simple for a person whose mathematical brain has not been stimulated. This dawned on me when Sheetal, a born-again mathematician, explained to me that in school, she had been taught to divide fractions by inverting the denominator and then multiplying it with the numerator.

What Sheetal meant was that if she were given a problem thus:

Problem: $\quad \frac{5}{4} \div \frac{4}{5} = ?$

She was told the method was:

Method: $\quad \frac{5}{4} \div \frac{4}{5} = \frac{5}{4} \times \frac{5}{4} = \frac{25}{16}$

She memorised the method but never understood it. Sheetal has an enquiring mind. Recently she decided to work it out for herself, and this is how she did it:

94

Problem: $\dfrac{5}{4}$ ÷ $\dfrac{4}{5}$ = ?

     (numerator)   (denominator)

Then she figured that the denominator $\dfrac{4}{5}$ had to be changed to $\dfrac{5}{4}$. She saw it as a number in itself and wrote it as:

$$\frac{4}{5} \times \frac{5}{4} = \frac{20}{20} = 1.$$

Dimly, she began to perceive the importance of this. So she wrote it down, inverting both fractions:

$$\frac{5}{4} \div \frac{4}{5} = \left(\frac{5}{4} \times \frac{5}{4}\right) \div \left(\frac{4}{5} \times \frac{5}{4}\right)$$

$$= \frac{25}{16} \div \frac{20}{20}$$

$$= \frac{25}{16} \div 1 = \frac{25}{16}$$

'Wasn't that rather a long process to get the same answer?' I asked.

'Of course it was,' she replied. 'But that is where I felt my maths teacher had turned us into robots. He never explained why we had to invert the denominator. But after working out several fractions using my method, I realised that what he had taught me was correct.'

I must have looked a little amused. She explained, 'Don't you see? My maths teacher was handing me a short cut. His intentions were good. Why teach the children this long-winded method when he could make life easier for us? He was handing us a finished product without explaining what went into the making of it.'

Suddenly I saw what she meant. But she insisted on giving me an example: 'I see all students as little "maths engineers". The teacher gives us a short cut, a bridge. But the next time we have to build a bridge on a different level, we will not be able to do it because we don't have the support system or the scaffolding to build it on. We don't understand it, so we cannot do it.'

Einstein and the little girl

I think you have understood what Sheetal meant. In fact, I have often wondered since, how much of maths we have to unlearn to learn it again! I think this point was understood by Albert Einstein. The city he lived in — Princeton — abounds with stories of this great man. One such tale is particularly striking, and I think you will enjoy it.

A little girl would often visit Einstein. Her mother, on realising what her daughter was doing, questioned her about it.

The little girl replied, 'I had trouble with my arithmetic homework. Someone said that at No. 112 lives a very big mathematician and that he is also a good man.' The mother listened with dawning horror as her little daughter continued artlessly, 'So I went to him and asked him to help me. He explained everything very well. I understood it much better than when our teacher explained it to us in school. He said I should come to him whenever I found a problem too difficult.'

Upset at what she saw as a presumption on her daughter's part, the agitated mother rushed to the hallowed No. 112 and apologised profusely for her daughter's behaviour.

Einstein said gently, 'You don't have to excuse yourself. I have certainly learnt more from the conversation with the child, than she did from me.'

I have often wondered if the great man realised the value of the 'scaffolding element' that Sheetal explained to me.

Avoid reinventing the wheel

Yet, I do realise that in maths certain things have to be taken as 'givens'. If a student had to spend time questioning and learning about every 'given,' he would never progress beyond a certain point. He might understand a few formulae thoroughly, but he wouldn't have more knowledge, only a limited store of it.

Therefore, I feel that you should approach maths from your individual point of view. For example, Sheetal's way of working out the problems may seem to you like reinventing the wheel. You know that to divide a fraction by a fraction, you have to invert the denominator and multiply the numerator with it thus:

$$\frac{2}{5} \div \frac{4}{3} = \frac{2}{5} \times \frac{3}{4} = \frac{6}{20}$$

It has not given you any trouble so far. It has become a part of you, so you may rightly feel that to follow Sheetal's method at this stage would be rather confusing. As I said, tackle problems that you haven't understood. Sheetal has her scaffoldings; you may require your own in other areas. Choose the ones that puzzle you and go on from there.

I feel that the 'missing link' between understanding and solving a problem often lies in one thing alone: the student has not understood the actual meaning of words like fractions, decimals and percentages. This is the reason why I started this chapter by defining each term and giving 'translated' examples.

It is just like learning to drive a car. Maths has different gears. When you reverse a car you go into reverse gear. The ability to 'reverse the mental gear' sometimes acts as a brake on the student. Maths gives problems that need a different gear or a different approach each time.

Let me illustrate this with a problem:

Problem:
In an examination, 75% of the candidates passed in English, 65% in Mathematics, while 15% failed in both English and Maths. If 495 students passed in both subjects, find the total number of candidates who took the exam.

To the maths-alien, this problem appears complex. But remember, percentages are there to *simplify* the matter. You will see what I mean as I give the step-by-step approach.

Method:
Suppose the number of candidates = 100,
75 passed in English. So, 25 failed in it.
65 passed in Maths. So, 35 failed in it.
15 failed in English and Maths.

Candidates failing in English alone =

$$25 - 15 = 10$$

Candidates failing in Maths alone =

$$35 - 15 = 20$$

So, number of failed candidates =

$$10 + 20 + 15 = 45$$

No. of passed candidates =

$$100 - 45 = 55$$

If 55 passed from the total of 100,

495 passed from the total no. =

$$\frac{100 \times 495}{55} = 900.$$

So, the total number who sat for the exam = 900

Percentage or a hundred, gives you a base or a yardstick to calculate the rest. Thus, 75% means 75 of every hundred. The last step may appear complex. But if you write it in words, it goes:

55 passed of 100

495 passed of X.

Now, assemble the 'passes' together. Next, put the totals together:

55 and 495; 100 and X

Then you put the ratio signs to make it clear.

55 : 495 : : 100 : X

This reads as, 55 is to 495 is the same as 100 is to X.

Translated:

Symbol	Meaning
:	is to
: :	is the same as

Once you have understood the relationship between the 'pass' and the 'total', the next step is easy. If 495 is multiplied by 100, it gives 49500 which cannot be the answer. When divided by 55, it gives the exact relationship to 49500.

Thus:

$$\frac{49500}{55} = 900$$

As Sheetal puts it: 'maths is like figuring out how you are related to such and such cousin and so on!'

Now do you see what I meant when I said relearning maths is very much like setting out on your first date? You have certain assumptions in your mind. You link them up elegantly. Before you know it, you are looking forward to your second date!

11

Mathability: Making it Easier

Turn your stumbling blocks into stepping stones.
ANONYMOUS

Over the years, I have talked to various people about maths. I find that most people face no problems with addition, subtraction and multiplication. But for some reason, division creates a slight setback. I have often wondered about this. One reason could be that students feel the different methods are taught in the order of difficulty. Addition being the easiest is taught first, followed by the slightly more difficult method — subtraction. Next is the more complex method — multiplication, and finally, the most difficult method—division.

This is not true. The sequence of teaching has nothing to do with which method is easier or more difficult. It is a natural progression. For example:

Subtraction is the reverse of addition.

Multiplication is a progression of addition.

In addition, you write:

$$2 + 2 + 2 + 2 = 8$$

In multiplication, it is:

$$2 \times 4 = 8$$

Here, the 4 denotes *4 times*. Hence, the tables we memorise are actually quick mental additions.

Division is the reverse of multiplication.

For example, in multiplication, you write:

$$3 \times 4 = 12$$

Here, you are adding 4 threes together. Thus:

$$3 + 3 + 3 + 3 = 12$$

In division, you write:

$$12 \div 3 = 4$$

Here, you are subtracting three 4 times:

$$12 - 3 - 3 - 3 - 3 = 0$$

I have given some elementary examples to give you a deeper understanding of these methods. Over the years, mathematicians have delighted in using their grasp of elementary principles to make maths easier still.

The 'tricks' of the trade

Some people are intimidated if they have to divide a number by 5. But they are comfortable with a round figure like 10. In such cases, they should take advantage of the fact that 5 is half of 10 and could do it this way:

Problem:		$165 \div 5 = ?$
Method:	1.	$165 \times 2 = 330$
	2.	$330 \div 10 = 33$
Answer:		$165 \div 5 = 33$

Similarly, if dividing by 15 poses a problem, remember that 15 is half of 30. Since 30 is a round figure, it might be easier to think in these terms:

Problem:		$105 \div 15 = ?$
Method:	1.	$105 \times 2 = 210$
	2.	$210 \div 30 = 7$
Answer:		$105 \div 15 = 7$

The simple logic here is that 30 is two times 15. So, if the dividend is 105, make it two times — $105 \times 2 = 210$. You already know that the divisor 15 when doubled is 30. In effect, you are doubling both numbers thus:

$(105 \times 2) \div (15 \times 2) = 210 \div 30 = 7$

So, $105 \div 15 = 7$

If you have to divide a number by 14, 16, 18, 20, 22 or 24, to simplify it to yourself, you can use numbers of lesser value such as 7, 8, 9, 10, 11 or 12.

Divisor 14:

Problem: $392 \div 14 = ?$

Using divisor 7:

Method:	a.	$392 \div 2 = 196$
	b.	$196 \div 7 = 28$
Answer:		$392 \div 14 = 28$

Divisor 16:

Problem: 464 ÷ 16 = ?

Using divisor 8:

Method: a.   464 ÷ 2 = 232

           b.   232 ÷ 8 = 29

Answer: 464 ÷ 16 = 29

The same method applies here:

1.   882 ÷ 18 =   441 ÷ 9 = 49
2. 4960 ÷ 20 = 2480 ÷ 10 = 248
3.   946 ÷ 22 =   473 ÷ 11 = 43
4. 1176 ÷ 24 =   588 ÷ 12 = 49

Dividing by factors

If you find it difficult to divide 1088 by 32, here is an easy method. You can break 32 into its factors. You know 8 × 4 = 32. So you can use 8 and 4 to divide 1088.

Problem: 1088 ÷ 32 = ?

Method: 1. 1088 ÷ 8 = 136

           2.   136 ÷ 4 = 34

Answer: 1088 ÷ 32 = 34

Or if you are given this calculation:

Problem: 2695 ÷ 55 = ?

Method   1.   5 × 11 = 55

           2. 2695 ÷ 5 = 539

           3.   539 ÷ 11 = 49

Taking the last example, you will realise how

105

much easier it is to do it this way rather than the way you were taught in school, which was:

$$5\,5)2\,6\,9\,5(4\,9$$

$$\underline{2\,2\,0}$$
$$4\,9\,5$$
$$\underline{4\,9\,5}$$
$$0\,0\,0$$

Of course, if you are at home using the school method, don't change it. My idea is only to make those of you who hit a mental block when faced with seemingly large numbers realise that there are easier methods of doing the same sum.

Let's take another example:

Problem: $8192 \div 16 = ?$

Keep in mind here that to divide by numbers that are power of 2 — such as 4, 16, 18, etc. — you have to halve only the dividend:

Method: 1. $8192 \div 2 = 4096$

2. $4096 \div 2 = 2048$

3. $2048 \div 2 = 1024$

4. $1024 \div 2 = 512$

To explain : $16 = 2 \times 2 \times 2 \times 2$. Or 2^4

So, by halving the number 8192 four times, you get the correct answer. Hence:

$$8192 \div 16 = 512$$

This technique is extremely useful when you are faced with a large number. For example:

Problem: 32768 ÷ 128 = ?

Method: 128 = 2 × 2 × 2 × 2 × 2 × 2 × 2.

Or 2^7

So, you halve 32768 seven times:

1. 32768 ÷ 2 = 16384
2. 16384 ÷ 2 = 8192
3. 8192 ÷ 2 = 4096
4. 4096 ÷ 2 = 2048
5. 2048 ÷ 2 = 1024
6. 1024 ÷ 2 = 512
7. 512 ÷ 2 = 256

Answer: 32768 ÷ 128 = 256

An important point to remember is that these methods work only with certain numbers. When given a problem, study the numbers involved. This will help you find a quick and easy way to solve it.

Dividing by fractions

This is an extremely interesting technique since it gives you an insight into fractions and how they work in division. Obviously, it is easier to divide by whole numbers than by fractions. What do you do if you see: $360 \div 7\frac{1}{2}$ = ?

There is a very easy way of doing it. Think. What is the link between the two numbers? What you want is a round number with which you are comfortable. As you think, you will realise that the first step is to make $7\frac{1}{2}$ into a round number. Try the numbers one by one. Discard those that don't suit you and take the one that you are comfortable with.

Making $7\frac{1}{2}$ into a round figure:

1. $7\frac{1}{2} \times 2 = 15$. Discard!

2. $7\frac{1}{2} \times 3 = 22.5$. Discard!

3. $7\frac{1}{2} \times 4 = 30$. Take it!

To equate the two numbers in the problem, multiply 360 by 4 too.

I will write it down step by step:

Problem: $360 \div 7\frac{1}{2} = ?$

Method: a. $7\frac{1}{2} \times 4 = 30$

      b. $360 \times 4 = 1440$

Now,   c. $1440 \div 30 = 48$

Answer: $360 \div 7\frac{1}{2} = 48$

Check list

There are certain simple tests that show whether a number is exactly divisible by another number — or a multiple of it. I have given them below for easy reference:

Number 2
If a number is divisible by 2, it will end in an even number or a 0.

Number 3
If a number is divisible by 3, the sum of its digits will be divisible by 3.

Example: Is 372 divisible by 3?

$$3 + 7 + 2 = 12.$$

Since 12 is divisible by 3, it means 372 is divisible by 3.

Number 4
If a number is divisible by 4, the last two digits are divisible by 4 or are zeros.

Example: Is 3188 divisible by 4?

$$88 \div 4 = 22$$

So, 3188 is divisible by 4.

Number 5
If a number is divisible by 5, the last digit will be 5 or 0.

Number 6
If a number is divisible by 6, the last digit will be even and the sum of the digits divisible by 3.

Example: Is 2076 divisible by 6?
a) It is an even number.
b) 2 + 0 + 7 + 6 = 15
c) 15 is divisible by 3
d) So, 2076 is divisible by 6

Number 7

Ah, this one has evaded mathematicians! There is no quick test to show if a number is divisible by 7.

Number 8

If a number is divisible by 8, the last three digits are divisible by 8.

Example: Is 4898760 divisible by 8?
760 ÷ 8 = 95

So, 4898760 is divisible by 8.

Number 9

If a number is divisible by 9, the sum of its digits are divisible by 9.

Example: Is 12122748 divisible by 9?
1 + 2 + 1 + 2 + 2 + 7
+ 4 + 8 = 27.
27 ÷ 9 = 3
So, 12122748 is divisible by 9.

Number 10

If a number is divisible by 10, it ends with a 0.

Number 11

This one is extremely interesting. How do you know if a number is divisible by 11?

Example: Is 58432 divisible by 11?

To work this out, add the digits in the even places, then those in the odd places.

The difference between the two answers should be 11 or 0.

Take 58432.

$$5 + 4 + 2 = 11$$
$$8 + 3 = 11$$
$$11 - 11 = 0.$$

So, 58432 is divisible by 11.

To divide by 10, 100, 1000 etc.

move decimal point one, two, three, etc. **places** to the *left* in dividend.

To divide by 0.1, 0.01, 0.001, etc.

move decimal point one, two, three, etc. **places** to the *right* in dividend.

To divide by $3\frac{1}{3}$

multiply by 3 and divide by 10.

To divide by $33\frac{1}{3}$

multiply by 3 and divide by 100.

To divide by $333\frac{1}{3}$

multiply by 3 and divide by 1000.

To divide by $16\frac{2}{3}$

multiply by 6 and divide by 100.

To divide by $12\frac{1}{3}$

multiply by 8 and divide by 100.

To divide by $8\frac{1}{3}$

multiply by 12 and divide by 100.

To divide by 25

multiply by 4 and divide by 100.

To divide by 50

multiply by 2 and divide by 100.

To divide by 125

multiply by 8 and divide by 1000.

To divide by 10, 100, 1000, etc.

move decimal point one, two, three, etc. places to the *right* in multiplicand.

To divide by 0.1, 0.01, 0.001, etc.

move decimal point one, two, three, etc. places to the *left* in multiplicand.

To divide by 5, 50, 500, etc.
multiply by 10, 100, 1000, etc.

To divide by 25, 250, etc.
multiply by 100, 1000, etc. and divide by 4.

To divide by 125
multiply by 1000 and divide by 8.

To divide by $33\frac{1}{3}$, $16\frac{2}{3}$, $12\frac{1}{2}$, $8\frac{1}{3}$, $6\frac{1}{4}$

multiply by 100 and divide by 3, 6, 8, 12, 16.

The methods I have outlined in this chapter can be called 'tricks', if you will! Why not? My purpose is to give you a 'scaffolding' to make it easier for you to divide. Such 'tricks' are used by the life-of-the-party type to enthral the guests with his or her 'mathematical prowess'! Try them out. It is all a part of the great maths-game! Instead of being intimidated, you can divide and rule!

12

Shorthand of Maths

Man is a tool-using animal . . .
without tools he is nothing,
with tools he is all.

THOMAS CARLYLE

Mathematics being such an intrinsic part of my mental make-up, I suppose I tend to take its usefulness for granted. However, a chance remark from a passing acquaintance jolted me out of my complacency.

A young lady who identified herself as Ashima, collared me at a party. 'I've always wanted to meet you,' she began. 'Tell me, why is mathematics in existence? Does it really serve any purpose?'

'Why do you say that?' I asked her.

'Well,' she said, 'except at a very elementary level, I don't see how it helps me in life. I mean, arithmetic is fine. But why do we have algebra? Couldn't we manage without it?' Before I could gather my thoughts, her escort appeared and took her away.

I too left the party. Her innocent remark had set me thinking and I wanted to be alone to sort out my thoughts. I thought of her words: 'Arithmetic is fine, but why algebra?'

The oldest language

To put it simply, I think mathematics in general is a revolution in the communication of ideas. It is a part and process of the evolution of mankind. And if you think back, it is the oldest language, the oldest philosophy in the world. By listening to sounds, man evolved the spoken language. Every region of the world had people expressing their feelings with sounds which became words. Later, language became a scientific process as we delved into its grammar. This evolution served a useful purpose as grunts were replaced by words to communicate better. As language flourished, it developed man's capacity for higher thinking.

To the early Indian sages, developing mathematics was yet another art, one more method of communication, one more way of understanding and relating to the world around them. We think that today we are in an era of specialisation. But I think our ancient sages were the original specialists. Their evolution was a constant, creative revolution. They were the original artists who explored the world and the universe through their senses. That is why they developed one more language — mathematics — and gave it to the world.

It caught the imagination of the people. Like any other language, it flowered as new ideas flowed into it. Take the English language, for instance. It has flowered and is constantly evolving because it absorbs new words from different environments. Indian words such as verandah and bungalow were assimilated into the English language only during the British Raj.

Mathematics flowered in the same way. Addition may have helped in the ancient barter system, enhancing a more 'blind' exchange of goods by giving them a certain value. Then a mathematical thinker worked out multiplication which, if you analyse it, is another way of addition, or a shorthand of addition. And just as any language has its roots in certain conventions and traditions, so does mathematics.

Lancelot Hogben, in *Mathematics in the Making*, describes the evolution of the positive or plus factors and the negative or minus factors. Taking the clock, he marked the top half as the positive arena, while the bottom half represented the negative arena.

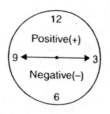

Perhaps tradition ruled that all maths calculations from 9 to 12 were of a positive nature, while 3 to 9 were of a negative nature. It is difficult now to figure out what functions our ancient forefathers had in their minds for each

116

symbol, each calculation. But then, we don't really know how every word evolved in, say, the English language. We don't even know why words spelt in the same way are pronounced differently. For example, notice the different pronunciations of 'put' and 'but'. Yet, we continue to use them as we have been taught.

Symbols and Signs

Maths too has certain ideas in it which cannot always be explained. For example, why do two negatives produce a positive? Perhaps the best answer is provided by Professor John T. Tate, a mathematician at Harvard, when he says: 'This rule is simply a convention that is universally agreed upon by people working with numbers because it is useful.'

That brings me back to the beginning. As I said earlier, maths was, and is, one more means of communication, one more language added to the human repertoire. Without maths we would be writing down ideas in longhand. We would be saying: 'Two plus three multiplied by two gives ten.' But using the shorthand way makes it easier:

$$(2 + 3) \times 2 = 10$$

It is *seeing* a calculation at a glance. It is a system, a symbolic language designed because it is convenient. If it weren't for the symbols and signs, we would have reams and reams on maths until finally it would be a dead science.

Fortunately, human brilliance keeps it alive. Ashima asked: 'Why algebra?' It is a little like asking: 'Why any other language? Why doesn't the entire world speak only one language?' Would we seriously want all languages, save one, to die out?

Simple equations as we know them today, were not so simple years ago. During the Renaissance, algebra was a very complicated process. For example, Pascal wrote it as:

Trouame. i.no.chegi$\overline{o}$ toal suo $\overline{q}$ drat.facia.12

Today, we know it as:

$$x + x^2 = 12.$$

Note the difference between a thought-process being written out in longhand, and the shorter, simpler way of modern algebra.

Later, a mathematician tried to simplify algebra by declaring that all vowels should stand for the unknown, while the consonants should denote the known. However, the great Descartes had the final word. Or, in this case, the final symbol! He decided that the last letters of the alphabet such as 'x' should stand for the unknowns and the letters at the beginning such as 'a' or 'c' should stand for knowns.

Now Descartes may have evolved this method either from a logical thought process or by some idea rooted in a certain tradition. The point is, as in any language where words have come down to us complete with their meanings, so has the symbol 'x' come to us meaning 'unknown'. We use it quite freely even in our everyday language. The x-factor representing the unknown is a commonly understood idea today.

Conquering the x-factor

Our ancient mathematicians had given birth to an idea. The next generation of thinkers set about polishing it or distilling it, and finally, boiling it down to a formula. With this formula, they could explore new areas and relationships.

We are the blessed inheritors of the simple equation, and are free to reach even higher if we want to. When we are taught algebra or any branch of mathematics in school, we are actually participating in the great growth of mathematics. Not all of us may specialise in it, but it helps us to explore our talents. That is why a good parent exposes the child to every possible discipline. For example, a child may have the potential to be a great tennis player, but if he is never exposed to the game, he will never know he has it in him. By exposing children to every field of maths, parents and educators are giving them the opportunity to grow.

In its simplest form, algebra is another version of arithmetic. You need not feel intimidated when you see a problem as:

Problem: $4x + 5 = 17$ Find x.

Again, it is common sense at work:

Method:
1. $(4 \times x) + 5 = 17$
2. Which number added to 5 gives 17?
3. $12 + 5 = 17$
4. $4 \times 3 = 12$
5. $4 \times 3 + 5 = 17$
6. $x = 3$.

Since you already know that $4x$ means $4 \times x$, the rest is easy. This may seem a long way of working it out, but our forefathers had to go through such long processes before they discovered a link and a formula was formed.

To understand an equation, look at it from a practical viewpoint. What is an equation? It is like a scale. The two sides should *balance* each other. So, when you look at an equation written this way:

$$x + 7 = 10$$

Visualise it on a scale:

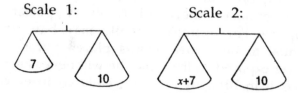

Scale 1:

7   10

Scale 2:

x+7   10

What is required to balance the scale?
It has to be $10 = 10$.
So you know that by adding 3 to 7 you get 10.

$$3 + 7 = 10 \quad x = 3$$

Give your intuition a chance

As you understand this fundamental principle underlying the equation, your intuition will begin to work. You won't need your visual scale to work out:

$$x + 24 = 34$$

You will know that x equals 10.

120

It is a simple matter of subtraction. If you keep the idea of balance in your mind, your natural intuition will take over, thus allowing you to grasp each idea faster and faster, until you feel you know it intuitively. When you see a seemingly more complex equation, the first question you should ask yourself is: 'What should I put on one side to balance the other side of the scale?' From this, you can go on to the more positive: 'To balance the equation, I must balance one side with the other.' This way you will be unfazed when you see:

$$x - 10 = 3$$

Here, I have deliberately made the figure on the right side of the equation a lower number, 3. But you know intuitively that x is 13, because $13 - 10 = 3$.

As the idea of *balance* becomes entrenched in your mind, your intuition will sharpen and your third eye will open wider.

What happens when you see the following problem?

$$10x = 5x + 10$$

How do you balance the two sides? You tackle it this way:

$$10x - 5x = 5x + 10 - 5x$$

Then, $$5x = 10$$

So, $$x = \frac{10}{5} = 2$$

What may set you wondering is that there is an x on both sides of the equation. But with the idea of balancing, you know you have to 'balance one side with the other.'

With this in mind, let's go on to the next step:

Look at this equation:

$$5x - 2 = 4x + 1$$

At first sight, it appears complicated. But it is not. First, see what you are comfortable with. You are happy with 2 and 1 because they don't have the unknown 'x' attached to them.

Now, decide which number you would like to use to balance the equation. Let's say, you decide on 2. What do you have to do to balance the equation?

You have to put 2 on both sides. So you write:

$$5x - 2 + 2 = 4x + 1 + 2.$$

Ah, isn't it already looking simpler? Now simplify it further:

$$5x = 4x + 3.$$

Go on with one more balancing act:

$$5x - 4x = 4x + 3 - 4x.$$

That gives you: $x = 3$ because all the x values cancel each other out. You have solved it with this understanding. Now, if you write it down step by step without the explanations, it would read:

Problem: $5x - 2 = 4x + 1$

Method: 1. $5x - 2 + 2 = 4x + 1 + 2$

2. $5x = 4x + 3$

3. $5x - 4x = 4x + 3 - 4x$

$x = 3.$

To give you a greater understanding of the workings of your mind, I suggest you formulate your own problem and work it out backwards. Suppose you start with:

1. $45 = 45$
2. $45 - 6 = 39 + 6$
3. $(15 \times 3) - 6 = (13 \times 3) + 6$
4. $15x - 6 = 13x + 6$.

If you toy around with numbers this way, you will get to know equations like the back of your hand!

With the next problem, keep in mind the idea of balancing.

Problem: There are two numbers with the difference of 3 between them. The difference of their squares is 51. What are the numbers?

Method:
1. One number is x
2. The other number is y
3. $\quad x - y = 3$
4. $\quad x^2 - y^2 = 51$
5. $\quad \dfrac{x^2 - y^2}{x - y} = \dfrac{51}{3} = 17$
6. That means, $x + y = 17$.
   Note: $x^2 - y^2 = (x - y)(x + y)$
7. $x - y = 3$. So, $17 + 3 = 20$
8. Since there are two numbers,
   $$2x = 20$$
9. So, $\quad x = \dfrac{20}{2} = 10$
10. $\quad\quad y = 7$.

123

As your intuition works on balancing every equation you come across, you will find that even the most complicated problem can be solved simply. In other words, you have conquered the x-factor!

13

Mathability: Human Face of Mathematics

Years ago, when I was young and inexperienced, if someone had asked me, 'What is calculus?' I would probably have bored them by talking like a mathematician! But experience has taught me that only by linking a subject to something the other person understands will the listener get the grasp of it. The comparison may not be a hundred per cent accurate, but it is sufficient to light that spark of interest.

If I were to tell you that calculus is about 'optimums' or 'rate of change', you would switch off mentally. But I remember telling somebody: 'Calculus is to maths what astrology is to astronomy.' Instantly, he was captivated. The description was not accurate, but it caught his interest. In fact, he held up his hand and exclaimed: 'Wait! Don't tell me. You mean that calculus finds relationships and analyses them?'

'Bingo!' I replied.

Director of maths

Since calculus has never been marketed, it is viewed with awe, or with indifference, or not at all! Yet, it is the extremely vibrant, very human face of maths. In calculus, you don't have to deal with numbers in themselves but with illustrations, such as shapes and graphs. It has an inbuilt technique. For example, a scriptwriter may write an excellent script, complete with a tight plot, strong characters, and effective dialogues. But that script will not be appreciated unless a director can bring it to life on the screen.

The director has the intuition and ability to fine-tune the script, highlight small details thus making them dramatic. He does this with a keen sense of awareness of what would appeal to the public. In other words, he is able to perceive the relationship between the written script, the way it will unfold on the screen, and audience appeal. That is what calculus is all about. It is the director of maths. It analyses and tunes relationships.

Take the hypothetical career of an Indian film actress. She is excellent at emoting, and is keen to take on varied roles. She gets three roles one after another, each different from the other.

The first role is of Sita, a beautiful and virtuous young woman. She will do anything for her husband, even walk through fire if he asked her to.

The second role is of Gita, a modern-day Rani of Jhansi. A fighter whose eyes flash fire and brimstone.

The third role is of Rita, a playgirl. She beguiles men, plays with their emotions, and discards them when she gets bored with them.

You will notice that I have taken three roles with extreme characteristics. To the actress, each role is a challenge as it calls upon all her acting prowess. With her immense talent she is poised for superstardom. But, in practice, does it work that way? If you were to plot a graph of her career, you would expect it to zoom steadily upwards. This is how her graph ought to look:

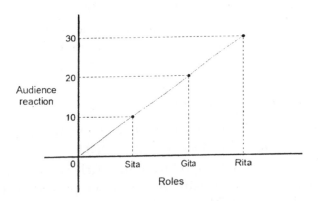

But in reality, this may not happen. Why? Because we have based our calculations purely on her talent. With each role she has excelled herself. But this is where the audience reaction sets in. So her graph will read:

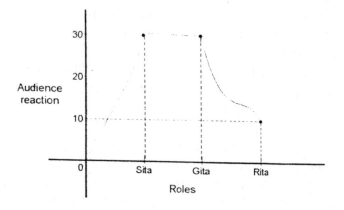

Why is there this unexpected downtrend? The key lies with the audience. They revered her as the pure Sita. They adored her as the gutsy Gita. But they hated her as the sly Rita.

In perceiving this relationship lies the science and art of calculus. This is where terms like 'infinite' and 'limits' come into calculus.

Calculus and the 'real world'

By now, I am sure you are beginning to understand this fascinating subject.

Some months ago I read an article about Asian workers. Traditionally, Asians have proved to be hard-working. They work twice or ten times as hard as non-Asians, at lower wages. Earlier, stricken by extreme poverty, they were even willing to work double shifts. Since they were paid by the hour, the more hours they worked, the more they earned. The word 'leisure' did not exist in their vocabulary. But with the improvement of their economic situation, came the gradual realisation that there was more to life than work. They discovered a life of leisure, of spending time with their families. So now, while they were willing to put in twelve hours, they were not willing to put in eighteen. They had reached their 'limits'. After a certain point, they valued leisure more than the extra money they could earn by working extra hours. Overtime was no longer that attractive.

This is where words like 'optimum level', 'limits' come in handy. This is where calculus takes over. The graph reads:

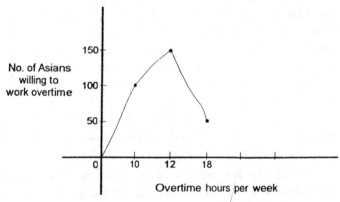

If you were to extend the graph to 20 or 24 hours, the curve would go lower. Such a graph would prove invaluable to an employer. From it he would be able to ascertain a pattern relating to the real world. The 'real world' perception is important because his paperwork would obviously show him the following:

1. His product has a vast, limitless market.

129

2. If his workers worked round the clock, he'd be able to get maximum production and maximum profits.

But, in practice, this may not work. His workers must be willing to work 24 hours, or he will have to employ more workers for night shifts. He will realise that such a situation hits a peak, but the human element begins to slowly lower it. The slope of the curve will help him to work out an optimum situation, thus enabling him to chart out the most efficient and effective system.

You may have noticed that both examples I have cited have a link. Both show the real world, the human element that runs so strongly in the best written project report. That is why I say, calculus is the vibrant, human face of maths. It has the inherent power to perceive and analyse a situation. An uninformed employer may think that the only incentive his worker needs is more money. But calculus will show him the human needs. Ironic, isn't it, that maths shows the human side to a human being?

Similarly, the actress may take on roles that are similar to the roles of Sita and Gita and turn down the Rita roles. You may mourn the fact that she has not explored her talent to the fullest, but the actress must weigh her inner satisfaction against box office success. Calculus makes her aware of the swings. It is up to her to choose.

This also holds true for, say, a shopkeeper. If he sets up shop in a competitive area, he will have to work out the optimum levels of sales to get a realistic picture. By careful study, he may find that he can succeed if he keeps his shop open later than the rest, or keeps it open on Sundays when others are closed. Perhaps, if he adds on a home-delivery service, he will stand a better chance of success. A maths-model clarifies the situation and enables him to find the peaks and the plateaus.

Finding relationships

Calculus also plays an important role in architecture. Erecting an effective dam or building has its roots in calculus. The architect works out his blueprint with an understanding of the precise relationship between forces. In effect, calculus catches the forces working on any given situation. Then it organises those forces. In the final analysis of these forces lies the key to the solution. The forces can be time, space, motion . . . .

Calculus helps in finding the area of different shapes. Most of us know that a square can be 2 cm. × 2 cm. = 4 sq. cm. or a rectangle 2 cm. × 4 cm. = 8 sq. cm. Here, we know that length × breadth = square area. But how do you find the area of a strange shape that does not conform to these set patterns? Take a swimming pool shaped like a piano, or the continent of Australia. Neither of them is a square, a rectangle, a triangle, or a circle. But by dividing the shape into several squares or rectangles, you can calculate its area. I won't go into technical details or the methods because I am not conducting a course in calculus through this book! What I'd like to do is to show you not just the usefulness or the relevance but also the human face of the subject.

Calculus has its own terminology which often makes it seem a difficult subject to tackle. For example, curved shapes are called 'functions'. To arrive at the human element, you will have to learn the science of it, grasp the concept. But once you have absorbed the basic idea of what calculus does and can do, you will no longer look on it with awe or indifference. Simply put, calculus is finding relationships. If you meet a new cousin, wouldn't you be interested in how he or she is related to you? Similarly, calculus is the family tree of maths. In its branches lie the fruits of efficiency and effectiveness.

14

Eccentricities of Maths

Genius means little more than the faculty of perceiving in an unhabitual way.

WILLIAM JAMES

As I write this chapter, I presume you have been reading the book in chronological order — chapter by chapter. You may or may not agree with everything I have said, but I am sure that you now view maths with more understanding and less fear.

In any field there is a degree of self-analysis. I know a writer who is so charmed by words that if she doesn't write her quota for the day, she feels unfulfilled. She says: 'Words turn me on. I see every day as a new birth in which I gather a bouquet of fresh experiences and thoughts.' Her ultimate nirvana is to write it all down by analysing what she has gathered and including it in her articles or stories.

Self-analysis can be fulfilling

I also know of a brilliant Indian classical singer. She is an interesting study. She feels she is beautiful only when she sings. When she was interviewed by a magazine, she looked forward to seeing herself in print. While the interview was on, the photographer kept circling her, photographing her in various candid poses. When the feature was finally printed, she was devastated. She felt she looked ugly in the pictures. 'I should have forbidden it. I should have asked them to photograph me at a solo performance.' She did not mean that she would look better because she was dressed for the show or had make-up on. What she meant was that being a true lover of music, it was only while she was singing that she achieved true beauty. This was when her very soul shone through in all its glory and made her beautiful. And this was the moment for the photographer to capture her on film.

I have captured such moments and thoughts and shared them with you to show you the wonderful art of self-analysis. Such an exercise carried out in moderation is extremely fulfilling. There is a romance to it and a sense of satisfaction. I want you to reach out and capture that warm, glowing, indescribable feeling and use it for maths.

Some psychologists believe that by delving into your past and examining, step by step, why you dislike maths, you will understand yourself and begin to like maths better.

I am the kind of person, however, who prefers to look ahead rather than back. Perhaps you can or cannot wipe out the past completely from your mind but, believe me, the best way to forget the past is to put it firmly behind you and look to the wonderful present and the glorious future. You can do it if you want to.

Let me assume that you have a comfortable lifestyle. It is immaterial whether you are married or divorced or whatever. You are fairly content with yourself. You have almost everything you need to meet your social, psychological, and bodily requirements. Curiosity or some other emotion has made you pick up this book. So now, let us look ahead.

Do you want to do maths? But maths for what? In this question lies the core of your self-analysis. Many people think that they should do maths only if they are planning to become mathematicians, engineers, or technocrats. That is like saying you should exercise daily only if you want to take up a sport professionally or become an athlete or a gymnast.

By being able to look at maths straight in the eye, you are able to take more control of yourself and of your life. It is amazing how much a small change in the pattern of life can do for you. Somehow, a little shift brings out the fighting spirit in you. As you learn to tackle one more area, you discover a 'plus' in you. In doing so, you have a great feeling of relief, of freedom, of having conquered something.

Demand the best from yourself

The best thing about starting something new is that your age doesn't matter. There is no time limit. You are not in competition with anybody. What is even better news is that since you are an adult, you have a rich store of experience, so you become a better mathematician because of what you have seen, heard, and done. Your ability to analyse is much sharper than it was when you were an innocent fledgling in school.

With absolutely no pressure on you, you can relearn maths by choosing the method that suits you best. There is no adult or authoritarian figure standing over you, demanding the impossible. There is no set procedure, no regimen involved.

If you are comfortable with words, you can work on it through sentences. If you find you enjoy numbers, you can discard the words. If you are a visualiser you can enjoy yourself by working on graphs or other diagrams.

In other words, what you are doing today is not learning or memorising a subject because it has to be done. Instead, you are taking on maths because you want to. You are seeing it as one more skill to be developed. Yes, a skill — such as playing table tennis or riding a bicycle or driving a car.

You can acquire and sharpen this skill in various ways. You can solve maths puzzles as you would a crossword puzzle. You can learn little 'tricks' to try on your friends. You can try out all those 'shortcut' methods that you couldn't in school. Oh, the potential is enormous!

Soaring high

Look on this phase of your adult life as: *All the things I couldn't do in maths when I was in school that I can do now.* You are now free to enjoy the peculiarities or eccentricities that are so typical of Old Man Maths. For example, take the number 8 and see what it does:

$$
\begin{array}{r}
888 \\
+ \quad 88 \\
+ \quad\ 8 \\
+ \quad\ 8 \\
+ \quad\ 8 \\
\hline
= 1000 \\
\end{array}
$$

You can imbibe the mystique of the number 9. Look at the multiplication tables:

$$9 \times 1 = 9$$
$$9 \times 2 = 18$$
$$9 \times 3 = 27$$
$$9 \times 4 = 36$$
$$9 \times 5 = 45$$

Now, add up the sum of the digits in each answer:

$$9 + 0 = 9$$
$$1 + 8 = 9$$
$$2 + 7 = 9$$
$$3 + 6 = 9$$
$$4 + 5 = 9$$

The sum is always 9!

Or take a number like 87594. Reverse the order of the digits: 49578. Subtract the lesser number from the greater one:

$$87594$$
$$- \ 49578$$

Remainder $= \overline{38016}$

Now, add the sum of the digits in the remainder:

$$3 + 8 + 0 + 1 + 6 = 18.$$

Again, add the sum of the digits in the answer:

$$1 + 8 = 9$$

So, it is back to King Nine!

It is a stimulating pastime. I am a great believer in spiritual harmony. I think that when you are absorbed in maths — which is the structure that our universe is built upon — you are in touch with yourself. You are in touch with your instincts, your heartbeats. And just as the singer felt that she was beautiful when she was singing, so it is with maths. It is when your spirit is stimulated that it soars on the wings of harmony.

15

Mathability: That Extra Step

If you want to do something, do it!
PLAUTUS

Why have I written a book on how to eliminate maths-alienness and encourage more people to take up maths? It is because I want to awaken within every reader the sleeping giant that slumbers due to ignorance or fear. That sleeping giant is 'Inspiration'. An unexplained, powerful, energetic force that, once awakened, gives you a great gift. The gift of willingness. The gift of action. The strong upsurge that makes you take *that extra step*.

Be an achiever

That extra step you take will make you an achiever. What is an achiever? A millionaire? A TV star? A politician? He is much more than that. An achiever is one who has accomplished something. A person who has attained his objectives. One who has overcome his fear. He does not have to be famous to be an achiever.

Every achiever — known or unknown — in the world is a successful person because he or she has taken that extra step. That is what I want you to do. You may already be a success in your chosen field. But if you overcome your fear of maths, you will be taking that extra step which will help you reap greater benefits and bring you joys that have so far eluded you.

Take the example of a farmer. He who takes that extra step and sows one more seed, pleases the great mathematician — Nature. She rewards him by multiplying that one little extra seed into several hundred grains. The farmer has one more achievement to his credit. He is blessed with a richer crop because he had the foresight, the willingness, the energy to take that extra step.

The benefits of maths

The benefits of that extra step are enormous. Let us examine them at a practical level and enumerate them. What do you gain by taking on maths?

- It makes you regard yourself with greater respect and in turn invokes respect from those around you.

- It provides you with greater opportunities for self-exploration and self-advancement.

- It compensates you by showing you another way of increasing your earning capacity.

- It makes you self-sufficient because you can plan your investments without any qualms.

- It leads you to develop your mind by adding one more accomplishment to your brain's repertoire.

- It protects you from job-retrenchment in difficult times, because you have an extra skill that might induce your employer to retain you.

- It enhances your job prospects because you possess that important skill.

- It makes you more aware, more alert, more keen because it is a constant source of inspiration.

- It develops initiative and enterprise within you, thanks to your new-found confidence.

- It gives others confidence in you and your ability.

- It banishes the old habit of procrastination that in the past prevented you from doing certain important things — such as balancing your chequebook.

- It gives you a purpose, an aim, a focus that insures you against restlessness.

- And finally, it makes you a recognised citizen of a wonderful new world — a world which follows the principles of the law of increasing returns. As I have said earlier, you have nothing to lose and everything to gain by learning maths.

Fling away those old, rusty fears.
Let your clean metal shine through.
Let your inspirational juices course through you.
Maths is your friend.
Maths is your instrument to a richer life.
Recognise the loyal friend who will never let
you down.
Give yourself a chance by giving maths a chance.
Maths has the answers, the solutions.
Take maths on and become an achiever.

Take that vital extra step!

16

Myths About Maths

W ho doesn't enjoy a bit of gossip? Film and
political personalities are its first target
almost anywhere in the world. Gossip adds spice
to life. There's something deliciously wicked about
it. Maths has its share of gossip too! Take a piece
of advice from me: enjoy it, then forget it. After
all, as Pascal put it so well, it boils down to two
plus two making five!

Let's have a cosy gossip-session about maths,
and then see what the real truth is behind the
gossip.

Myth: Women mathematicians are masculine.

Truth: Who says so? Do you think an intimate
knowledge of the magic of numbers
makes women suddenly sprout bristles
on their cheeks? No way. In fact, as

far back as the 60s, American researchers came up with the startling revelation that women mathematicians were 'significantly more feminine'!

Myth: Non-mathematical males are sissy and feminine.

Truth: Rubbish! Is there any medical proof for this? But this senseless allegation makes the poor non-maths male feel as if he has gone in for a sex-change operation! He is ashamed to admit that the only 'pi' he relishes is Mom's Apple Pie!

Myth: When it comes to maths, you have to lock up your intuition and let pure logic take over.

Truth: Tsk, tsk! Without intuition where would logic be? For example, you've watched a murderer commit a crime; then he tries to convince you in a logical way that you never really saw it. Despite his persuasive arguments, will you be convinced? Of course not! Heed the wise words of one of the greatest mathematicians the world has ever produced: 'To these elementary laws (of physics) there leads no logical path, but only intuition supported by being sympathetically in touch with experience.' It was Einstein himself who came to this conclusion!

144

Words like 'rational', 'precise', 'logical' have given poor Old Man Maths a bad name! Yet mathematical history points towards intuition. Newton intuitively knew calculus existed somewhere on the fringes of the consciousness of mathematics. But he couldn't devise the logical steps required to give flesh and blood to the skeleton of his idea.

In mathematics, intuition is the parent of invention. Logic follows like a well-trained dog. In fact, maths does not have its roots in logic at all. It is rooted in ideas to make life more practical, more organised. Those ideas are born out of observation and intuition. René Descartes, who has been given the awesome title of 'Father of Modern Mathematics', was one day idly watching a fly crawl on the ceiling of his room. His intuitive mind caught an idea that made him chart the path of the fly in maths-lingo. And analytical geometry was born! It depends on what and where your mind is tuned to for that moment. The Scottish king Robert Bruce deduced an entirely different philosophy from watching the spider!

An industrialist who wants to set up a new plant may ask for data, profit and loss projections, and so on, from his marketing men. They may come up with a picture that proves that the new project is going to be a financial disaster. They may advise him through this logical process not to go ahead with it. But if his intuition tells him otherwise, he will use their projections to evaluate the risk factors and still go ahead. The eventual success of the project is not due to logic but to his intuition!

Each one of us has this special mathematical intuition within us. We have to learn to listen to it.

Myth: Approximate is for the birds, exactness is for mathematicians.

Truth: Well, well, well! I'd rather be a bird in that case! Of course, exact answers do help, but only at scientific laboratory levels. Take heart from the fact that 'approximate' is what we live by in any field. When you tot up your grocery bill, you needn't do it to the last *paisa* or cent. A once-over, just to satisfy yourself that it's not wide off the mark, is enough. Even maths-oriented knowledge hinges on the approximate. The distance from the earth to the sun is *approximately* 150,000,000 kilometres. The surface area of the globe is *approximately* 500 million kilometres.

It is only in school that you are taught to get exact answers at the simple arithmetic level. This is because you are being taught a skill and should learn to be as perfect as possible at that point of time. But later, there is no real value or satisfaction in being accurate to the last digit. For example, in a project report a figure such as 3.65 is rounded off to 3.7, and so on. So, it all depends on the circumstances. Even a doctor says that if his patient is over fifty-five years of age, a blood pressure level of about 140 to 150 is fine.

Myth: If you count on your fingers, you are a philistine!

Truth: Pooh! For some reason, counting on the fingers is not seen as 'elegant'. Yet, many .do it under the table, behind their backs, and so on. What parents and teachers have to understand is that there's nothing wrong with counting on the fingers. What is the abacus after all? It is a slightly more advanced way of counting on the fingers. Strangely enough, the constant use of a calculator is not as frowned upon as counting on the fingers. A calculator only makes you lazy and robs you of the ability to calculate on your own. Counting on the fingers doesn't. And as I've said earlier, maths began at our fingertips, so why the new inhibition?

Myth: The faster you solve a new problem, the smarter you are.

Truth: Yes, if you are planning to compete against Carl Lewis in a 100 m race! Mathematicians are no more speed merchants than are writers. A good writer can take years to write a novel. Here, speed is not essential. So also in maths. Speed proves nothing, absolutely nothing. What counts here is experience and practice. A classical singer makes her performance look so fluid, so effortless, but it is hard work, practice, and experience that make this possible. So is it with mathematicians. Pen and paper are required. The time mathematicians take depends on their experience — whether they've solved similar problems before. If there is a variation, their intuition too comes in handy. And don't forget that special person — Lady Luck!

So don't get discouraged and throw up your hands if you come across a problem that looks tough. Just pick up the pen, think, and start!

Myth: You have to have the memory of an elephant to be a good mathematician.

Truth: If that were so, elephants would be good mathematicians! Think of it this way: when you begin to learn the English language, you have to first memorise the alphabet, but as you go on, it becomes a part of you. This includes grammar and vocabulary. Similarly, with maths you should allow the symbols and the practice of them to become a part of you. After all, doesn't 'two plus two equals four' roll easily off your tongue?

What is maths? It is the same as any language. You have to understand the concepts in it just as you have to understand the grammar in a language. Grammar has rules; and maths has formulae.

Unfortunately, from an early age we are taught to rattle off multiplication tables like parrots. Few children grasp the concept of tables — that $2 \times 2 = 4$ is the same as $2 + 2 = 4$, or that $3 \times 3 = 9$ is the same as $3 + 3 + 3 = 9$.

I have an amusing incident to relate with regard to tables. About to knock on the door of my friend's home, I noticed that it was slightly ajar.

Planning to surprise her, I pushed it open fully, but stopped when I heard this conversation between her and her ten-year-old son:

'Where are you going?'

'To play.'

'Have you learnt your sixteen times table?'

'Yes, Mummy.'

'All right. Recite them to me. I want to hear them.'

'Can't I recite them later?'

'No. Right now.'

Pause. Then the boy's voice started in that sing-song manner. It went: 'Sixteen-ones-are-sixteen! Sixteen-twos-are-thirty! Sixteen-threes-are-forty-five!'

He paused to take a breath and my friend said, 'Very good! Go on!'

Unable to suppress my laughter, I walked in. Looking sheepish, the boy stopped. Obviously, he neither had the interest nor the understanding of the tables. He was reciting the fifteen times table to his mother who didn't know any better!!!

Such incidents bring home the fact that people think tables and other mathematical concepts are to be memorised, not understood. Yet, in any field only by understanding do you remember. Even the lyrics of a song are remembered better if you have understood the meaning of the words. That is why some people say they are 'word-deaf'.

In maths, a proper grasp of the basics is essential. This grasp helps as problems become increasingly complex. Memorising a formula won't help if you haven't understood the application of it.

Myth: There's no flash of inspiration in maths. It's all perspiration!

Truth: If that were so, why did Archimedes jump out of his bath, yelling the now famous word 'Eureka'? That's because he had a flash of inspiration. Both these qualities are required to solve maths problems.

Myth: You either have the ability to do maths or you don't. Mathematicians are born, not made.

Truth: For mathematicians, what a lovely image to have! If this were true, they would be on cloud nine, with people looking at them in awe for their special 'inborn' abilities! But the truth is that one is not born a mathematician. It is an acquired skill, a skill that can be taught to everyone. But the false idea

150

that mathematicians are born not made, raises mental barriers for most people. They tell themselves: 'I can't do it because I was not born with a maths brain.' As they go on repeating it, they undermine their own self-confidence.

Believe in Yourself

Maths is exactly like a sport. If a sportsperson feels she can't better the world record, she'll never do it because she has not geared herself for it. Negative emotions stop her from even trying. Oh, you may see her running on the track, but her heart won't be in it. So also with maths. Believe in yourself, believe you can do it and you *will* be able to do it. If it comes to that, I'd say we are all born to maths, but we don't know it.

Now that you have read about the *myths* what for it is, I hope you will be able to discard any false notions you may have about maths. It's a great companion and has all the requisites of life in it — work, fun and games, and even myth!

Awaken the Genius in Your Child
Shakuntala Devi

Your child's achieving attitude begins with you.

Teaching your child is important. Teaching your child to think is more important. Thinking is not information or knowledge or being right. Thinking is the skill which unlocks the potential within. It is the essential difference that separates winners and achievers from others.

This book will help you — the caring parent — combine the unique knowledge of your child's personality with the latest research on how children learn at each stage — infancy, pre-school and through school. At every stage, the book will help enhance your child's concentration skills, problem-solving abilities and creativity — the complex dynamics which translate a child's potential into a brilliant legal mind, a gifted surgeon or a path-breaking physicist.

'The human computer, Shakuntala Devi, says geniuses are nurtured, not born. She even tells you how.'
India Today

... the book is a must for all parents.
The Statesman